GOVERNORS STATE UNI
P9-DJK-725
3 1611 00217 4271

The Reflective School Counselor's Guide to PRACTITIONER RESEARCH

I would like to dedicate this book to Mike McNamara and Ruth Shagoury for their encouragement, support, and belief in the work we do on behalf of children.

—Vicki Brooks-McNamara

I would like to dedicate this book to Irma, Camilo, Emma, Santiago, and Marco, whose natural curiosity always leads to good questions.

—Danielle Torres

The Reflective School Counselor's Guide to PRACTITIONER RESEARCH

Skills and Strategies for Successful Inquiry

Vicki Brooks-McNamara
Danielle Torres

For information:

Corwin Press
A Sage Publications Company
2455 Teller Road
Thousand Oaks, California 91320
www.corwinpress.com

Sage Publications Ltd.
1 Oliver's Yard
55 City Road
London EC1Y 1SP
United Kingdom

Sage Publications India Pvt. Ltd.
B 1/I 1 Mohan Cooperative
Industrial Area
Mathura Road, New Delhi 110 044
India

Sage Publications Asia-Pacific Pte. Ltd.
33 Pekin Street #02-01
Far East Square
Singapore 048763

Printed in the United States of America

Library of Congress Cataloging-in-Publication Data

Brooks-McNamara, Vicki.
The reflective school counselor's guide to practitioner research:
skills and strategies for successful inquiry/Vicki Brooks-McNamara,
Danielle Torres.
p. cm.
Includes bibliographical references and index.
ISBN 978-1-4129-5109-8 (cloth)
ISBN 978-1-4129-5110-4 (pbk.)
1. Educational counseling—United States—Handbooks, manuals, etc. 2. Student counselors—United States—Handbooks, manuals, etc. I. Torres, Danielle. II. Title.

LB1027.5.B7352008
371.4—dc22 2007014590

This book is printed on acid-free paper.

07 08 09 10 11 10 9 8 7 6 5 4 3 2 1

Acquisitions Editor: Stacy Wagner
Managing Editor: Jessica Allan
Editorial Assistant: Joanna Coelho
Copy Editor: Monica Burden
Typesetter: C&M Digitals (P) Ltd.
Proofreader: William H. Stoddard
Indexer: Sheila Bodell
Cover Designer: Lisa Riley

Contents

Acknowledgments

The authors would like to acknowledge and graciously thank Dianne Wilson and her school district, Tigard-Tualatin in Oregon, for allowing us to provide an ongoing case study at the end of each chapter. Without the district and Dianne's feedback and support, the book would not have been given the real-life journey of pursuing the difficult questions and answers.

The authors would like to acknowledge the work Sue Reynolds brought forth in the initial development of what was to become this book. Sue's contributions to the overview of content and writings in the first chapter helped bring the book to reality.

Corwin Press wishes to thank the following peer reviewers for their editorial insight and guidance:

Deryl F. Bailey
Associate Professor
University of Georgia
Athens, Georgia

Stephanie A. Bierman, NBCT
School Counselor
West Lake Elementary School
Apex, NC

Karen M. Joseph
School Counselor for the Highly Gifted
Roberto Clemente Middle School, Upcounty Center for the Highly Gifted
Germantown, Maryland

Yvonne Katz
Superintendent, retired
Consultant to School Districts
San Antonio, Texas

Todd E. Ryan
Director of Guidance and Counseling
Louisa County High School
Mineral, VA

Angie Stansell
School Counselor
Hatton High School
Muscle Shoals, AL

About the Authors

Vicki Brooks-McNamara received her PhD in counselor education from the University of Wyoming. She taught all K–12 levels before becoming a school counselor and counselor educator. Under Vicki's leadership, the school counseling program at Lewis & Clark College in Portland, Oregon, transformed into a premier program preparing school counselors to be leaders and advocates who are guided by data to facilitate systemic change.

Vicki currently is a senior consultant with the Education Trust. She coordinates and facilitates district and statewide school counseling workshops to assist practitioners in essential skill development necessary in today's school reform. She was on the editorial board of the *Professional School Counseling* journal for six years and is a Senior Fulbright recipient. She is a consultant and advisory member for the College Board's National Office of School Counselor Advocacy. Vicki resides in Portland with her husband Mike.

Danielle Torres earned a BA and an MA from Pepperdine University and a PhD in Counseling Psychology from the University of Oregon. She is currently a faculty member of the School Counseling Program at Lewis & Clark College in Portland, Oregon. Her teaching includes courses in action research, diversity issues in education, and the professional development of school counselors. She has experience as a counselor in schools at all grade levels and with various school-based research projects. Dr. Torres resides in Portland.

Introduction

If we knew what it was we were doing, it would not be called research, would it?

—Albert Einstein

SCHOOL COUNSELORS COLLABORATING FOR HIGH STUDENT ACHIEVEMENT

Positively impacting school culture and enhancing learning are central to the work of educators. School counselors can partner with educators while utilizing practitioner inquiry to support high achievement and learning for all students.

Historically, school counselors have worked in isolation. However, twenty-first-century school counselors must include in their professional work membership on leadership teams, advocating for all members of the educational institution, using data to guide and inform daily practices, and collaborating to create systemic change. School counselors are ideally positioned to conduct *systemic practitioner inquiry*—that is, working extensively outside of the classroom, seeing and hearing the larger learning community as a whole—even if, at times, they'd rather not be aware of what they see and hear!

Research conducted by educators in the field is vital, and school counselors are no exception. We must continuously question and evaluate daily occurrences in our schools. Only by asking questions, gathering data, and allowing ourselves to be informed as a community of learners will we continue to provide high quality learning for all students.

We believe this is the only guidebook *specific* to practitioner inquiry for school counselors. Teacher inquiry provides wonderful insights for the classroom. Missing are questions targeting the larger learning community. School counselors have long recognized the importance of asking difficult questions. What has not been readily apparent is (1) how to frame and ask the questions, (2) how to gather authentic data, and (3) how to use results to create lasting systemic change. Practitioner inquiry for school counselors embraces more than gathering data about students. In the larger context, school counselor practitioner inquiry can encompass the entire school and/or community and reach beyond the school counselor's everyday work in the building. Practitioner inquiry for school counselors can best be defined as a quest or journey to better understand the issues pressing on the system that potentially create barriers for students.

SCHOOL CULTURE IN THE TIME OF SCHOOL REFORM

We write this book in the midst of school reform. Many elementary, middle, and high schools are being placed on remediation lists. We watch as morale plummets in the buildings, parents voice frustration, and state legislatures mandate yet one more layer of bureaucracy for all school personnel to decipher. Despite all of the apparent negatives, we find educators embracing their profession, continuing to evaluate their work while designing and implementing creative, thoughtful, and engaging learning experiences for students. School personnel continue to come together and defy the odds: students *are* demonstrating achievement far exceeding the bottom line. Schools *are* making the national roster for closing the achievement gap (Chenoweth, 2007).

We have been fortunate to work with committed professionals who believe in themselves, their students, and their transforming schools. A culture of caring, concern, and genuine commitment is repeatedly demonstrated by educational professionals. Culture is a direct result of hard work and continuous effort by all stakeholders, extending beyond the school building to include the community as a whole.

Partnerships have been developed in new and exciting ways between schools and communities. These partnerships bring individuals from all walks of life together for a common goal: educating all students to high standards. A common thread can be identified in partnership success: collaboration between all stakeholders. We have been fortunate to have Laura Pedersen, school counseling program coordinator at Lewis & Clark College, share her expertise on building stakeholder partnerships in Chapter 6. This chapter provides strategies that will enable you to reach out successfully to all potential members of your community.

TIPS FOR USING THE BOOK

A side note to the writing of this book: We began the journey after learning of the need for the text from school counseling practitioners and counselor educators. As we began the work, we struggled with the idea of research versus educational research versus inquiry. We were aware of the reluctance, and even fear, that many educators have when it comes to doing "research." This is why our book title encourages readers to begin the journey of becoming researcher-practitioners in their schools. After soul searching and evaluating existing writings, we chose to guide school counselors to undertake their data and research endeavors through the lens of *inquiry*, a user-friendly word without the negative connotation so many educators attach to the word *research.* As David Hagstrom wrote in *From Outrageous to Inspired*, "The way of inquiry evokes participants' understandings, values, and intents, as well as their gifts and talents. Taking the way of inquiry allows the group to become the leader in the school community" (2004, p. 91).

We have designed this book as a practical tool. We realize some chapters may be of more interest than others. For example, Chapter 2, Discovering the Territory: Exploring Others' Expertise, might not be essential to your question as a practitioner but might be more essential for pursuing potential solutions. Do not hesitate to peruse the book and find chapters or sections speaking to your current work or area(s) of concern. An ongoing case study at the end of each chapter highlights the salient points with a hands-on example of how it can be done.

We hope this book will assist you and your fellow professionals in mutual discovery of essential questions to very real and pressing issues, concerns, or questions you may have in your school. We wish you well in your journey—and we would love to hear your stories!

Launching Inquiry 1

Developing Your Question

Research is a high-hat word that scares a lot of people. It needn't. It's rather simple. Essentially research is nothing but a state of mind . . . a friendly, welcoming attitude toward change . . . going out to look for change instead of waiting for it to come . . . an effort do things better.

—Charles Kettering

The word *research* can instill anxiety in many people. Memories of graduate school and statistics may come to mind. In this book, we will call our journey in finding answers *practitioner inquiry* (PI). Why call it PI rather than research? In PI we can use existing data; our everyday work can lead us to seek answers to the questions arising from our interactions with students, faculty, and parents.

HOW WE ARRIVED AT THIS POINT

School Reform

A closer look at the real world of schools can lead to genuine change to better serve our school communities. So let's step back for a minute and review the school counselor's role in the educational system and the school reform movement. Initially, school counselors were ancillary to the school reform issue. Conversations took place and decisions were made without any involvement of the school counseling department. However, as the issues continued to press on the school and stakeholders began to look deeper into the issue facing the reform movement, the school counselor or school counseling department began to surface as the one knowing the overall picture of the school and community. No one in the building hears more, sees more, or knows more about students, faculty, staff, parents, and the community than the school counselor! School counselors must be included in school reform on a level conveying a clear message: their help and support are essential in this journey.

Research or Inquiry?

To fully collaborate in the school reform journey, school counselors need to understand and embrace the use of data. The data may already exist within the system. On the other hand, it is likely that questions will develop requiring new data to determine essential and appropriate next steps.

Rather than expecting outside researchers to come into the schools, we can use existing data (e.g., test scores vs. passing grades, course enrollment patterns) or we can gather data from daily issues and concerns (e.g., How many students are absent in the first few hours of the day?). This is the heart of practitioner inquiry: asking the very real and difficult questions.

Using Existing Data

Schools are filled with data: dropout and graduation rates, test scores, attendance, disciplinary referrals, and enrollment patterns of students' selection of courses, to name a few. Everywhere you look the educational culture provides a rich arena of data. According to Ruth Johnson (2002):

> Data can provide tremendous food for thought in schools where low expectations lead to low results for large numbers

> of your people . . . most often low-income students of color. These are the first kinds of data schools should examine to absorb the troubling implications of tracking and other status quo practices. . . . data can begin to illustrate the gaps between words and actual behaviors in many schools. (p. 14)

PI seeks to gather existing data to inform us to move to a question, which is so much simpler than trying to create your own research study! Just look at your school's available data, and you'll see it's virtually impossible not to start asking questions.

MOVING INTO INQUIRY

Inquiry is a natural and important part of our professional practice. In our jobs, questions constantly arise as to why something happened or how an issue can be addressed or changed. During his first year as a school counselor in 2002, Ian Martin started keeping a research journal, which had been one of the recommendations in his preservice courses. Individuals were encouraged to write down questions they had about how they might improve something in their schools. His first entry follows:

> Where do I begin? I must first report on where I am: struggling through my first year as a school counselor and trying to keep my head above water. I consider getting through the day as a major success.
>
> Along those same lines exists the beginnings of my questioning. Over the last couple of months I have been collaborating with another staff member to create an after school program. She is a Special Education teacher focused on academic results. She wants to establish a non-fiction reading program. I on the other hand, hope to operate in the more creative vein of art. Our thinking is that by combining the two disciplines we can create a balanced experience that addresses the concrete and abstract elements of both practices.

> As a counselor I am constantly communicating the relationship between academics and creative expression. This opportunity allows me a chance to back up my words. Will we see an increased interest in reading? Will students become more comfortable expressing themselves through art? Will they begin to combine both tools through synergy? How will we collect the data? Is there a relationship between fact and fiction? Will students become more creative as their factual thinking becomes more sophisticated? Will their images become more realistic? These and many more questions get me excited about this project.
>
> There is an interesting byproduct that I feel I have to mention. That byproduct is excitement. I know that my day is busy and I probably don't have time to tackle another project, but the concept has me wanting to explore. All of the stories that we hear on the radio or on T.V. about exceptional teachers and students result from people that are motivated to learn. There is a thirst, a vision, and a goal to learn more. That thirst is why I entered this profession. It is key in keeping me motivated, because like it or not, we are educators and students. The more that I experience, the more that I feel that true educators never stop being students. I am motivated and invested in my education and I am proud to say that I am learning every day. I hope to look back on this journal and compare these ideas in relation to where I finally end up. Who knows where that might be? This is my kind of research! (2002)

How do we tap into Ian's enthusiasm and move into practitioner inquiry? First, we encourage Ian to gather any relevant data on his students, from test scores, attendance, and homework completion to teachers' observations (e.g., during instructional time, lunch, an assembly). From this, he can begin to develop questions. Perhaps he wonders: What happens to nonfiction reading abilities when I introduce the students to artists and use their media to illustrate nonfiction books? Whatever he chooses to inquire about, it will be a clear reflection of the questions he really wants to explore. From this, Ian will think about how and where he will look for and gather data.

DATA SOURCES

Locations for data can be many and varied. From your building to national centers, we can find data in many locations. Let's look at various entities where data may be accessed.

State Department of Education. Data abounds in the state department, from test scores to district demographics. Check out your State Department of Education's Web site; you will find a plethora of information and data specific to your building as well as to your district and state. For example, on the North Carolina state department Web site (www.ncpublicschools.org), there is a tab titled Statistics/Data. By clicking on that tab, you can find further information under several categories: About NC Schools, Student Testing Results, Student Testing Information and Results, Evaluation/Analysis, and the Accountability Division. By clicking on Student Testing Results, you can then select from a variety of reports. Table 1.1 shows just one example of data on student testing results that can be accessed via the state department Web site.

School District. Your school district can provide substantial data to help inform your inquiries. Before searching your district's Web site, think about your school in relation to the district. Do you have programs with a particular focus? Are your school demographics different from other schools in the district? What does your school board require? On what aspects of learning has the district placed its emphasis? What does the school district articulate as short- and long-term goals?

Building. What data is already available in the school? How is data on courses and programs collected? What data currently exists on the achievement, discipline, dropout, referral, or failure rates within your building? What additional needs are evidenced within your school? What questions arise because of the uniqueness of the school itself?

We often forget simple things done every day. What about bus referrals? Attendance? Schedule changes? Time spent in classroom instruction? How about truancy? ESL/ESOL services? What behaviors or data are regularly tracked? Does your school compile three-, six-, or nine-week failing reports?

Table 1.1 Hudson Elementary School, End of Grade (Reading) Composite Grades 3 Through 8: Detailed Gender-Ethnicity, Migrant, Free/Reduced Lunch and Limited English Proficiency Status Breakdowns

	2003–2004			*2004–2005*		
Student Subgroup	*Number at or Above Level III*	*Number of Valid Scores*	*Percentage at or Above Level III*	*Number at or Above Level III*	*Number of Valid Scores*	*Percentage at or Above Level III*
Female—Hispanic	8	9	88.9%	≥ 95.0%	8	≥ 95.0%
Female—Multiracial	*	1	*	*	0	*
Female—White	172	186	92.5%	153	166	92.2%
Male—Asian	*	0	*	*	1	*
Male—Black	*	0	*	*	1	*
Male—Hispanic	11	12	91.7%	8	11	72.7%
Male—Multiracial	*	2	*	*	1	*
Male—White	140	171	81.9%	135	166	81.3%
Free/reduced lunch	119	149	79.9%	125	154	81.2%
Not free/reduced lunch	215	232	92.7%	182	200	91.0%
Limited English proficiency	8	9	88.9%	4	6	66.7%
Not limited English proficient	326	372	87.6%	303	348	87.1%
Not migrant	334	381	87.7%	307	354	86.7%

Note: The percentage and number of students are not shown if the percentage is greater than 95 or less than 5. Subgroups with no data are not shown in this table.

* Student population in subgroup too small for value to be reported.

As you can see, the range of data is seemingly endless. However, what is lacking are the initial questions to begin the quest in using data to derive solutions.

THINKING ABOUT THINKING

How would you define *metacognition*? Simply put, it's thinking about thinking. Most of us have a particular way in which we think. Some think in concrete terms, which require specific details to complete the picture. Others of us might think in abstract terms, without specific details. Whatever your modality of thinking, inquiry needs to support it and help you think in new ways. If inquiry occurs only in the area or method in which you are comfortable, essential information and feedback could be overlooked. Learning, thinking, reflecting, and sharing information can occur in a multitude of arenas. We must be open to exploring the information as it is presented even when it is out of our comfort zone. For example, Student A may have linguistic talent that readily catches our attention. Student B's talent might lie in interpersonal intelligence, while Student C's learning is best correlated with bodily/kinesthetic interactions. These examples come from Howard Gardner's (2006) multiple intelligences work and provides a strong argument for exploring our thinking and understanding via many avenues.

Some of us will rely on hard factual data while others use written notes or recorded conversation as the primary way of gathering information. Still others will use outside resources whether it be individuals or written material. And yet others would much rather observe and take notes (either in written or taped format), then reflect on the information at a later date. No matter which method you prefer, it is wise to remember that information is given and received in multiple venues.

FORMULATING QUESTIONS

Some school counselors catch the fever of questions and become passionate question machines. Adam Swientek is a middle school counselor known for writing his way to understanding. Adam's writing brought him to this draft of his questions:

Main Question:

- What are the social and academic developmental implications that former ESL/ELL students experience when making the transition from a self-contained shelter classroom to an inclusive classroom environment?

Subquestions:

- What is the self-esteem of the students in their new classroom environment?
- Are the students comfortable with their new instructors? Do they feel that they have an outlet or can reach out for assistance?
- Are the students able to assimilate into the classroom, develop friendships with students of different ethnicities or race, and believe they belong to a social group?
- Do students sense a different, positive educational experience?
- Are there outlets that the former ESL/ELL students can go to for assistance in the classroom or outside of the classroom?
- Has the students' identification to their race or culture changed because of a new, modeled environment?
- Are students more compelled to complete middle school and high school because of the mainstreaming?
- Do students have an urgency to attend postsecondary college or take up a vocational trade because of the impact of transition? (2002)

This was a great outpouring of Adam's questions, and yet he realized he had even more that he wanted to explore!

EXPLORING YOUR QUESTION

Selection/Identification. Begin by selecting a student, issue, or concern. Often we select a child who takes a lot of our time: a name frequently heard in the faculty room or written on bus referrals. We encourage you to consider a child you don't know well. Perhaps it is a child who doesn't come to school until 9:00 a.m. Does your student have an older sibling? Family health issues? A single parent? Are there other students who are also consistently late to school? Are there commonalities among these students? Where do they live? Do they have a low income?

Form 1.1 is a case study worksheet. Think about an issue in your school that needs particular attention. You can use the worksheet to help you determine

- What are the facts?
- What else do you need to know?
- What are possible sources for additional information?

Keep a close check on the assumptions you may begin to make. Do you really know the truth of what you write down? Work on your objectivity with fierce determination. You'll have time later to follow hunches.

What do you want to know? Once you have identified the area, issue, or students you would like to know more about, think about what you already know. What questions begin to bubble up? Be open to *anything* popping up into your head! Do they even care about being in school? Are their parents home at night? How many other students also have afterschool jobs? This last question was asked by a high school counseling department when a large number of students regularly missed first- and second-hour classes.

What else do you need to know? Look at your list of questions. Where can you find the real information? The cumulative files? Talking with the teachers? Parents? Coaches? Will you take time to observe or talk to these students during recess or lunch? After disaggregating their first- and second-hour absences by ethnicity, the counseling department was able to see the majority of students were Hispanic. The counselors began by talking with students during lunch. After all, they were at school during the lunch hour!

Form 1.1 Case Study Worksheet: Template

Concern/Issue/Question: ______________________________

What are the facts?	*What do you want to know? What else do you need to know?*	*Possible sources for additional information*

What are possible sources for additional information? The first two categories will lead you to this arena. Here is where you will explore other possibilities for resources, information, or data. Do other teachers have similar students? Do the ESOL or Special Education students face similar struggles? Does the district office store school longitudinal data? Are community members deeply involved with the school? How about the graduates?

Let's continue with our Hispanic students missing first- and second-hour classes. The mere fact that the majority of absences occurred in the Hispanic population during first and second hour led the counselors to begin to look at the daily schedule. What implications for missing the classes might exist for these students?

STRATEGIES FOR SUCCESS

Anyone can become an educational inquirer by pursuing one question at a time! It demands a willingness to be informed by the questions arising in our minds. We are often trained to put aside our questions, wonderings, or ideas. School counselor Liz Mahlum (2003) wrestled with the concept of practitioner inquiry from the first class meeting. Continuing to focus on the finished product—what was she going to prove—she struggled with the concept of "being in the question." Toward the end of the class, Liz wrote about her process of finally "getting it."

> After struggling through the development of my question and being able to differentiate between data collection and analysis, I got it. I was finally being forced to think about my thinking. I was challenged to step away from deadlines and actually think about the "how" and the "why" ahead of time. This has been uncomfortable. Hidden in the discomfort, however, was an opportunity for me to assess the time that I spend with students and whether or not I am taking advantage of the abundant opportunities for change that they present to me on a daily basis.
>
> In actuality, uncovering and igniting a spark of curiosity is quite simple. Even today, as I talked to a student, I just couldn't

help but wonder "What if . . . ?" In a brief 20-minute conversation, he made my wheels turn. I wasn't hunting for a research idea, but what he shared with me made me wonder. It was simple and concise, but could easily be an area worth exploring. At that point, I recognized that research doesn't have to be huge; in fact it might be small but nonetheless important. (2002)

Meet Dianne: An Ongoing Case Study

Dianne Wilson, a working practitioner, is our focus for the Ongoing Case Study section of each chapter. Dianne worked with children in county mental health and day treatment settings for many years and then decided to become a licensed school counselor. She has been a practicing school counselor for eight years. During that time, she has helped move the faculty and staff perception of the school counselor's work from ancillary to an essential service central to the work of the entire school. No longer is she viewed through a lens of "What do you really do?" In partnership with her administrator, she has restructured her role to include being a key player on the leadership team.

So let's begin Dianne's PI journey, how it came to be, and what motivated her.

The Issue

Dianne Wilson, an elementary school counselor in Tigard, Oregon, provides this example of using data to drive her practitioner inquiry.

> Under the new rules of school reform, we test third and fifth grade students. A large number of third graders were failing the tests. It really didn't matter who was the teacher; the scores still indicated they couldn't perform up to state standards. It was obvious we needed to develop some academic interventions to help these students. We knew asking parents to monitor homework wouldn't work because a large percentage of our students are from low-income, single-parent families. And a lot of the parents are working two jobs, so no one is home to help!

This sounds familiar to many of us who have worked in similar schools: high numbers of at-risk students having little or no support from home. Even some staff and faculty members have the attitude, "It will never change." However, Dianne was motivated to step outside the norm and dig for a deeper understanding of what was happening to these children and why. She knew she had become a school counselor because she wanted to make a difference in students' lives. That difference had to first begin with helping *all* children achieve academic success—after all, she was employed by an educational institution! Her work in the private setting led her to the realization that without a strong education, the children were headed for a lifetime of struggle.

Many times it takes one individual who will go against the flow, be obstinate, and look "outside the box." One obvious tactic Dianne might have taken would have been to partner with the teachers to bolster the academic rigor of the assignments for students with failing scores. However, as you will learn in this ongoing case study, approaching the issue in that manner would have been less effective than the manner she chose. There was much going on behind the scenes.

Given the information Dianne was presented with, what would you have done? Where would you have begun? Whom would you have approached? Were there any other sources of information that could have proven beneficial? As we move along in the book, you will begin to get some "ah-has" as to potential options in this situation. Using Table 1.2, let's begin to fill out the columns as Dianne might have. Let's see what you can add to the list and where your inquiry might take you.

Table 1.2 Case Study Worksheet: Poor Third Graders' State Test Performance

What are the facts?	*What do you want to know?*	*Possible sources for additional information*
77% of Grades 3 and 5 combined met reading benchmarks. 65% of Grades 3 and 5 combined passed writing. 72% of Grades 3 and 5 passed math multiple choice. 62% of Grade 5 passed math problem solving. This was below where we wanted to be as a school.	• Who are the teachers? First year or seasoned? • Who are these students? • Where do they live? *What else do you need to know?* • Curriculum for all? Same? Different? • Do they have siblings? • What do you know about their parents' financial/personal situation?	• Teachers • Parents • Siblings • Community contacts

2 Discovering the Territory

Exploring Others' Expertise

At this point, you may have a wonderful and exciting practitioner inquiry project ahead of you, but you may be wondering about its importance, relevance, or direction. There is an entire world of information out there that can help substantiate your idea and lead to new ways of planning your next steps. This chapter discusses the purpose and methods of exploring others' expertise, which is both the foundation for your research and the gateway to your project.

WHY GATHER SUPPORTING INFORMATION?

As a consumer of products, whether they are educational or not, you probably appreciate reading reviews that discuss the quality and nature of the product rather than just taking the seller's word for it. With practitioner inquiry, the idea is similar: you want your reader to grasp the importance of the topic, understand the landscape of the topic, and appreciate the benefits of addressing the topic. You can do this by gathering information that has already been collected and summarizing it in your own format. There are essentially three steps: (1) gathering relevant literature, (2) reading the literature, and (3) writing a summary of the literature. Writing a summary at the start of your practitioner inquiry project may appear to be a time-consuming undertaking, but there are several benefits.

EXPLORING OTHERS' EXPERTISE

While there are a number of reasons to become familiar with the work others have done, we've identified four core benefits.

A Sense of Knowing What Is Going On "in the Field." To establish your inquiry project as valid, it is important to convey that you have solid knowledge of the issue being explored. You will quickly learn that reviewing others' work on the same or a similar topic provides a sense of understanding various aspects as you get to know it from different angles. Reading others' work will expose you to some of the historical information (e.g., what has gone on previously in this arena), central findings, and major influences. You, in turn, will write a review of the material you come across, thereby summarizing the scope of your topic and demonstrating that you do indeed have the essential background information needed to launch your idea.

Insight Into How Others Have Addressed the Problem. As you read information describing problems addressed by others, you will also discover measures that have been applied and evaluated. You may gain a new perspective for addressing the problem you are exploring: How did other schools address the same problem you have identified as an issue in your school? What specific methods were implemented and did the results point to success or failure? What aspects of their plan would they recommend doing differently or the same? Authors of published research frequently include suggestions for future consideration that may coincide with ideas you are considering for your project.

An Understanding of the Factors Involved in Cause and Effect, Correlations, and Other Associative Relationships. Reading about previous investigations allows you to observe relationships. How do others describe their findings and to what do they attribute their conclusions? What other factors seem to influence or have an impact on the issue you want to explore? It is important to ask yourself, How do I go beyond common sense associations of the topic I am addressing? For example, it seems logical that dropping out of high school would be associated with lower earned wages over a lifetime, but where is the evidence for such a claim, and how strong is it? Many educators comment they have observed a significant increase in diagnoses of ADHD in children over the last 10 years, but where is the evidence, and how much of an increase has there truly been, if any? Is it really sensible to think that small class size has a positive impact on learning for students, and why would we draw that conclusion? Previous research will provide you with a foundation to substantiate your claims for the importance of your topic and the factors surrounding it.

A Model for Your Own Practitioner Inquiry Project. While others' work can contain helpful information, it can also serve as a model of organization and writing style as you begin to design your own practitioner inquiry project. Notice the way others have planned and carried out their studies. How did they inform their decisions as they developed and implemented their project? What did they consider as they selected the participants, setting, data, and evaluation aspects of their study? What sorts of data indicators did they select for their particular topic? How did they access, analyze, and discuss data? How did other authors write about their topic, their projects, and their findings? What voice do they utilize in their writing, and how might the audience differ from study to study? Are there consistencies in the organization of material you are reading and reviewing? How do you as a reader respond to the different writing styles and content, and what do you prefer? The more you read, the better ideas you will have to carry out, write up, and present in your practitioner inquiry project.

As you can see, reviewing others' expertise is an important aspect of your entire practitioner inquiry project; you can glean helpful ideas from previous work that can be implemented in your own project. Also, the written component of your project articulates critical background information for your chosen research topic. Let's discuss the steps to a quality search for information.

KEEPING IT SIMPLE

While we are going to go into detail about the various methods and resources for locating information to use in guiding your work, we know one of the basic rules of the practitioner inquiry process is to keep the project simple and relevant to your needs. With that said, there are no requirements as to the amount and type of information you need to support your journey on this topic. Yes, your exploration will be more scholarly if you use a large number of refereed journal articles (journals in which articles for publications are reviewed by scholars in the field) and books. But is that what you want or need for your practitioner inquiry project? Perhaps all you need is information regarding previous research pursuits in this area, a few supporting articles, and a few examples of others' data to create a foundation to frame your project. Know the eventual audience and the purpose for your project, balance your available time and resources, then make decisions about the amount of research you need to gather. You will need to explore others' work in your area of concern to substantiate and convey a rationale for your project, but the extent and scope are up to you.

In the next sections, we'll walk through three important steps in gathering your project's supporting literature.

Step One: Gathering Others' Expertise

There are many places to begin looking for supporting information for your project. Consider exploring statewide resources for locating material to incorporate into your review. Look for publications provided by your State Department of Education or public and private organizations known to do work related to your topic. Literature might be in the form of

- Brochures
- Published reports
- Newspaper articles
- Web pages
- Policy papers

Professional conferences also abound with information from various presentations and other forums where research is shared among educators.

Literature from national and/or global stages is primarily accessed using two resources: the Internet and libraries.

The Internet. Due to the time constraints of working school counselors and other educators, the Internet is often the first place to turn to when searching for information. The growing access and ease of use, not to mention the vast amount of information available online, make the Internet an essential tool for obtaining resources. A good place to start looking for previous information on your topic is to use an online search engine, such as Google, Yahoo, or Dogpile. There are also Web sites that may be of particular use to educators, such as the federal Department of Education (http://www.ed.gov); the Educator's Reference Desk (www.eduref.org), which provides thousands of educational resources including counseling and family life categories; the No Child Left Behind Web site (www.ed.gov/nclb); The Education Trust (www2.edtrust.org), which provides statistics and information on achievement gap issues and state-to-state comparisons of academic achievement; the American School Counselor Association (http://www.schoolcounselor.org), which maintains an archive of publications and other information for members; and Teaching Tolerance by the Southern Poverty Law Center (http://www.tolerance.org), which shares tools for teaching about diversity in schools. These and other Web sites may point you in the direction of your specific topic.

It is important to keep an open mind when using the Internet as a resource. You will need to pay attention to the various links and recommendations of other resources that may also provide the information you are looking for in your field of interest. The Internet has an enormous collection of information, so it is easy to feel overwhelmed or lost when searching within it. You will undoubtedly make a few wrong turns and hit a few dead ends (see Box Tips 2.1). The key is to be patient, stay alert, and return to the few Web sites that are your favorites for the specific topic you are researching.

Box Tips 2.1 Evaluating Quality Web Sites

Within the endless universe of Internet Web sites, there is quite a range in the quality and content of various online resources. How is one to determine the good from the bad?

Here are a few questions to pose when surfing the Web for research-based resources:

- What person or organization is responsible for disseminating the information posted on the Web site? Is it from a highly recognizable entity or well-known expert?
- What is the process for posting information on the Web site? Are there likely several reviewers ensuring the quality the content before it is posted, or is it a "free-for-all" that allows anyone and everyone to post information?
- How comprehensive is the Web site? Is it dedicated to a particular field, and does it offer links and options to other perspectives within the same general topic?
- What is the purpose of the information? Does it appear to be academically rigorous and objective, or is it casual and subjective?
- How well written is the information? Was time taken to ensure a professional publication, or are there visible mistakes and errors, giving it a haphazard look?
- Does the research you encounter include the original citations that would allow you to locate the same resources for yourself?
- What do you know about the person or organization posting the information? Are there funding sources or supporting bodies with other associations that might bias the information posted?
- Did you find the information helpful? In what ways could you utilize the information to support your practitioner inquiry?

Libraries. Your local public library is a great place to explore for books, newspaper articles, and other media resources. Public libraries use catalog databases containing records for every book and resource held in their building. In addition, most libraries also have an interlibrary catalog system displaying the contents of other area libraries. Patrons can order and borrow resources from other libraries via an interlibrary loan system.

A specialized place to search for literature is at a college or university library. College libraries are even more helpful to educators than public libraries because of the databases available through subscriptions purchased by the college. These databases are collections of journal articles, papers, dissertations, book chapters, and books from fields such as education, psychology, biology, or political science. They are organized by field, which increases the chances you are looking for literature in the right place from the start, unlike the Internet. School counselors and educators often find that databases such as ERIC, Education Full Text, and PsycInfo are among the most useful for locating information in their field. Legal databases may come in handy if you want to look into an ethical or legal topic (e.g., special education, confidentiality, discipline).

These databases provide the user with a list of references matching the search criteria the user inputs into a template of categories (e.g., dates, keywords, authors, or title names that help to narrow down the search; the amount of information used as search criteria is up to you). See Box Tips 2.2 for ideas to help you navigate a successful search and increase the likelihood you generate a helpful list of references. You can then locate the actual document from online, from the library shelves, or from an interlibrary loan system involving additional regional libraries. Increasingly, these databases provide *full text* resources, which means the entire article or document is available online, and with a click of the mouse you can read it on the screen or print a copy for yourself.

Box Tips 2.2 The Key to a Successful Literature Search

When searching a library catalog for previous information to help inform your work, you will likely use the search criteria features of databases. This allows you to insert information to narrow your search and increase the chances that you find material that is on target with your chosen topic.

One such criterion is the *keyword search* option, permitting you to type the key words, or main vocabulary, that would most likely be found in the literature you are seeking. Say, for example, that you are looking for the topic of "using study skills groups to decrease the number of ninth graders failing one or more classes." What might be the key words contained in the articles, books, or papers that you would like to read on that topic? Maybe *study skills, ninth grader, class failure*?

It seems logical, but many educators find that a keyword search can be among the most helpful and, at the same time, the most frustrating tools in a database search. The issue is that often the keyword you think might be the key to unlocking an extensive list of reference hits isn't the same key programmed into the mind of the database. Sometimes, using "ninth grader" as a key word won't yield any hits, but using "high school students" will produce a multitude of hits. Be patient, be aware of the most commonly used vocabulary in the field, and ask for assistance from a librarian to brainstorm alternative words to use in your search.

So what kind of information would be most helpful for your work? There is no single answer to this question because it depends largely on your topic, your question, and the search resources at hand. Let's discuss the main types of information you may come across and the most likely places to find them.

Journal Articles. Journal articles are primarily written synopses of studies or discussions of previous research conducted by professionals in the field. They are printed in journals, which are collections of writings by various authors published in a timely manner, such as monthly or quarterly. There is a wide range of quality and content across different journals, and each journal has its own criteria and process for selecting the articles to be published; some are quite rigorous, while others are less scrupulous. In addition to research studies, journal articles also offer writings on topics of interest to professionals in the field, such as a historical perspective, a write-up of field observations, suggestions for best practices, or an editorial-style piece of writing. Journal articles can often be located via the Internet on the journal's Web site or anywhere hardbound journals are available for reading (e.g., libraries, professional centers).

Books and Book Chapters. Books and book chapters can provide in-depth writings on a broad topic. Some books are authored by a single author in a single voice, while other books are edited, meaning the editor(s) enlist various authors to write individual chapters on a specific topic falling under the scope of a larger topic. Books are also helpful because they may contain additional appendices, such as glossaries, chapter summaries, and extensive resource lists, pointing you toward even more potential information. Books related to educational topics are usually found in libraries, in bookstores, through textbook publishers, and online. Peers and colleagues may also be a source for borrowing books on particular topics.

Published Reports and Papers. Many organizations and professional bodies develop reports or papers and disseminate them to professionals in the field. These writings may speak to issues large and small. They may provide details, updates, or recommendations for new directions in education. These types of publications require a critical eye as to the purpose and source of the writing; there may be a motive for the development of the report leading you to question the merit or objectivity of the writing. Nonetheless, published reports and papers can be extremely valuable documents for use in your background exploration. These are most often found online and in hard copy form from the original organizational or publishing source.

Magazine and Newspaper Articles. These types of articles are snapshots of contemporary issues of the day, often written with a subjectivity and brevity making for interesting and easy reading. While magazine and newspaper articles are not considered rigorous scholarly material, they do provide useful supplemental information. National magazines often profile educational issues from various perspectives, while local newspapers usually describe issues affecting the immediate geographical area. Both may contain worthwhile background information, descriptive statistics, or anecdotal accounts of the topic you are reviewing. Magazines can be difficult to locate unless the publisher keeps a thorough archive of past issues. Newspapers are usually archived regularly either in a library or within the publishing company, although you may be required to purchase copies rather than obtain them free. One suggestion is to maintain a file of appealing educational articles that you come across, cut out, and put away for future use.

Step Two: Reading the Literature

Now that you have gathered the relevant research, reading it all may seem like a daunting and detail-oriented process. The goal in reviewing others' work is to build links between the past and your present practitioner inquiry idea. Keeping this in mind will help you sift through the reading in a timely and purposeful manner.

We have developed a list of questions to help guide your reading and help you readily identify the most useful information for building your case. While the questions do not pertain to all information sources, they do offer starting points for reading and reflection.

As you read, examine the literature for the following information:

1. Determine the type of literature and where it comes from (e.g., journal article, book chapter, magazine article, manuscript, review, brochure).

2. Is there a summary at the start or the end of the document (e.g., an abstract, introduction, synopsis, or outline) providing an overview of the reading? If yes, read it first to determine if it is relevant to your topic.

3. How is the main topic defined or described, what does it look like, or what does it mean according to the author?
4. How do the authors build support and summarize background information throughout the reading?
5. If it is an article that describes a study, what did the study involve (e.g., participants, setting, instruments, data analysis, results) and how were the hypotheses resolved? For more suggestions for reading research studies specifically, see Box Tips 2.3.
6. For other types of reading, what were the main ideas addressed and what kind of details were provided that appealed to your interest in the topic?
7. What evaluation methods were developed or implemented to address the main topic?
8. What did the authors conclude at the end of the reading?
9. What do the authors recommend or suggest to improve professional practices?
10. Did the reading have any statistics or descriptors that support the importance of the topic that you want to address in your research?
11. Are there aspects of the writing style that you particularly enjoyed? Perhaps the organization and composition were easy for you to follow or the graphics helped you understand the findings. Could you use some of these same writing strategies to convey your ideas when you write up or present your project?
12. After reading all of the literature you have gathered, think about the logical connections among the sources. How are they consistent or not? Do they start to naturally connect or do they separate into various categories? How might you use them in your literature review?

Box Tips 2.3 Guidelines for Critically Reading a Journal Article

These tips assume a basic knowledge of reading and understanding research studies, whereas the rest of this manuscript does not take any knowledge for granted.

- Read the abstract and determine whether the article is relevant and appropriate for your practitioner inquiry topic.
- Determine whether the study described is experimental or not (was anything manipulated?).
- Determine whether the study is quantitative (objective) or qualitative (subjective).
- Determine if procedures were appropriate (e.g., subject selection, group or number of subjects, group distribution, length of study).
- Determine if there is sufficient information regarding the measures or instruments. A thorough article will include a description of the instruments, the administration procedures, the training procedures, the testing procedures and scores, the validity and reliability of information, and steps the researchers took to minimize concerns for bias in the study.
- Make a list of the basic findings from the results section. Reread this section or add any notes that help you understand the meaning of the results. It may be helpful to focus on the big ideas before you tackle the numbers and statistics.
- Read the discussion section. Are the implications discussed valid? Are the implications relevant for your research? Are there any implications that were not addressed? Did the author(s) address any limitations of the study? Does your research idea fit in with any of the proposed future research?
- Last, highlight any relevant articles cited in the reference section. This is a great way to find additional pertinent articles that you can then retrieve and read for yourself.

Step Three: Writing the Summary

As you embark on writing your literature review, let's consider the major purposes of the written summary:

- To define any main terms or key concepts important to your practitioner inquiry project
- To discuss and compare particular points you observe in others' work as they relate to your project
- To point out the strengths and limitations of the previous work
- To include ideas relevant to your proposed practitioner inquiry project idea
- To build a case for your practitioner inquiry project
- To show that you have an understanding of existing work that informs your practitioner inquiry topic
- To identify your own community of scholars (Where do you fit philosophically within the landscape of the topic and with whom do you align?)

It is also important that you know some of the basics as you start to write the summary. Be sure to know the expected use for the finished summary. Is it going to be part of a lengthy or brief write-up of your entire project? Will it be reviewed by a school board or school administrators? Will it become a presentation to a particular audience? Is it an assignment for a course? Do you hope to publish your practitioner inquiry project eventually? Think of your written summary as a way to present your ideas logically and professionally to the reader, whether your audience is your school community, a professor, or a publisher. A 2005 preservice student wrote the following summary of her inquiry of others' work in her area of interest, predictors of college attendance. Specifically, she was interested in exploring the number of students taking the PSAT in her particular school.

> It is evident from past research that there are many variables that one can examine to predict a student's likelihood to attend college. One common component throughout these predictors is the role that guidance plays in helping students achieve school success as well as post–high school success. Ideally, a student will find guidance from parents, peers,

teachers, counselors, and various others throughout their school experience thereby strengthening their academic potential. Unfortunately, research illustrates that a large percentage of our students are not receiving adequate guidance. As school counselors it is our job to plant the seed of high expectation and academic success in all of our students. One way to do this is through encouraging students to participate in taking the PSAT in order to help them see college as a long-term goal. (Matteri, 2005)

COMPONENTS OF THE SUMMARY

Introduction

The introduction should address the following:

- What is the purpose of your practitioner inquiry project idea?
- Why is your practitioner inquiry topic important, in general?
- What is the goal of your practitioner inquiry project?
- What are the benefits of your practitioner inquiry project?
- What is your passion for your practitioner inquiry project?

Main Body of Summary: Others' Expertise and Your Project

The body of the summary should address the following:

- Define any main terms or key concepts important to your project.
- Discuss, critique, and compare particular points you observe in others' works.
- Point out the strengths and weaknesses of the previous studies. Refer to Box Tips 2.3 for ideas when reviewing an article.
- Articulate and support the themes and major findings.
- Describe the relationships between factors found in others' work.
- Mention the most frequently cited studies and worthwhile groundbreaking studies.

- Address important historical issues of the topic, describe trends over time, and end with contemporary issues involving the topic.
- It may be helpful to write in a way that organizes the information and builds support from the material you gathered. You may want to ask yourself these questions:
    1. How does this topic impact individual children or adolescents?
    2. How does this topic impact the school community, including students, teachers, counselors, staff, administrators, parents, school boards, or school districts?
    3. How does this topic impact communities or society at large, and what might be the long-term consequences or implications associated with the topic?
    4. What solutions have been developed or implemented to address this topic? What are examples of ideas, programs, interventions, or important considerations utilized by other schools? What are the goals or outcomes of solutions cited in the previous literature?
    5. What diversity issues should be considered?
    6. What achievement gap issues should be considered?
- Remember to stay focused by writing about ideas relevant to your proposed project idea. If it isn't relevant, don't write about it.
- Keep in mind that you are assembling the informational summary to establish support for your action project idea. Arrange the literature review so that it flows well and is coherent.

Conclusion

The conclusion should

- Briefly summarize the big concepts, main themes, and consistencies you found during your review of others' information and data.

- Give an overview of the major ideas and point toward future directions for the topic.
- Demonstrate you have a solid understanding of the project topic.
- Set up your practitioner inquiry project, sensibly tying your project idea with the information you have reviewed and presented.

Exploring others' expertise should be a thoughtful and careful process, from the search to the reading and finally to the writing. It is the foundation of your project, a proclamation of the many logical considerations substantiating your project as a necessary and constructive endeavor. A sense of confidence and validation is the sign of a well-written summary. You have now paved the way for the remainder of your practitioner inquiry project.

Dianne's Journey Begins

How did Dianne explore others' expertise? She followed the KISS principle: keep it simple Sally. She knew volumes of educational strategies existed in the field for students who were underperforming on tests. However, Dianne's intuition told her that this issue was beyond the development of student-focused interventions (e.g., study skills groups) and needed to include a wider audience. She began to look beyond the individual students and to listen to what others had to share from their perspective.

Her previous professional experiences tugged at her to think about family and community influences on students' lives. The supervision class for her licensure program was reading *Common Purpose* (Schorr, 1997). Many of the discussions in the book were readily applicable to what Dianne was experiencing with the discerning data. Something seemed to be telling her that this was bigger than an intervention led by one person but she couldn't quite put her finger on it.

What more did she need to know about the students? Were there issues in the classroom? Between students? Between teacher and student(s)? Dianne visited with her colleagues about their insights into the students and their poor test performances. After her discussions, she began to view the data through a different lens and began to formulate some additional questions. Where did the failing students live? Exactly what was or was not going on in the homes? How many students had no supervision before or after school? Were there other individuals who had similar concerns? Who in the community might be able to provide some insights? To begin to find answers to some of these questions she talked with administrators, faculty, and the liaison to the Community Partners for Affordable Housing. The liaison was able to give Dianne some much needed insight into the community at large as well as contact information and suggestions for how to work with the individuals and groups in the community. Thus began a journey that would prove to have a positive impact on both the school and community.

Getting It Together 3

Gathering Your Data

Data need not scare you. The word *data* can be a user-friendly term, signaling an assessment of current or recent events. Yes, data can be test scores or dropout rates, but data can also be the pieces of quantifiable information guiding and informing our work. So let's not struggle with the word *data* any longer; let's embrace the information it can provide in leading us to best practices. If we can follow two easy and simple steps, we can manage data and make data work for us—ultimately, the benefactors will be the students.

Step Number One. Get organized by prioritizing and narrowing the fields. This means taking the data and assessing what is and is not important. For example, if our data is the number of all failing students in the seventh grade, we might consider disaggregating the data by subject, gender, socioeconomic status (SES), or ethnicity. From the smaller groups, we can discern potential areas to target, for example, African American females. Or we might further define failing as one or more D's or F's. Thus, the data that at first appeared to be overwhelming has now become manageable and is rich with possibilities for strategic and systemic interventions.

Step Number Two. Focus and identify the issue. Using the failing seventh graders as an example and disaggregating the data by gender and subject area, we might learn that the females failing math far outnumber the males. We have now narrowed our focus from all failing seventh graders to females failing math, and then to the disproportionate number of African American females failing math, a more manageable pool from which to begin considering next steps.

ETHICAL CONSIDERATIONS

As school counselors, it is our charge to use data to address issues of inequities in our schools. Our role is to support students by serving them fairly, providing equal access to opportunities, and advocating for systemic changes when current practices create barriers for some students (Stone & Dahir, 2004). If the school counselor does not become the voice of underrepresented students and families, who will? Our ethical responsibility to our students, programs, and schools is clearly stated in the American School Counselor Association's (ASCA, 2005) ethical standards as follows:

> **Accountability Position Statement:** Professional school counselors use data to show the impact of the school counseling program on school improvement and student achievement.
>
> **Preamble:** Each person (student) has the right . . . to a program that advocates for and affirms all students from diverse populations. Each person has the right to receive the information and support needed to move toward self-direction . . . with special care being given to students who have historically not received adequate educational services.
>
> **A.1. Responsibilities to Students:** The professional school counselor: (b) is concerned with the educational, academic, career, personal and social needs and encourages the maximum development of every student.
>
> **D.1. Responsibilities to the School**
>
> a. Supports and protects the educational program against any infringement not in students' best interest.

b. Informs appropriate officials in accordance with school policy of conditions that may be potentially disruptive or damaging to the school's mission . . . while honoring the confidentiality between the student and counselor.

A.3 Counseling Plans: The professional school counselor: (v) advocates for counseling plans supporting students' right to choose from the wide array of options when they leave secondary education.

A.9 Evaluation, Assessment and Interpretation: Assesses the effectiveness of his/her program. . . . through accountability measure especially examining efforts to close achievement, opportunity and attainment gaps.

D.1 Responsibilities to the School: The professional school counselor: (a) supports and protects the educational program against any infringement not in students' best interest; (g) assists in developing . . . (2) educational procedures and programs to meet students' developmental needs and (3) a systematic evaluation process for . . . programs, services and personnel.

E. Responsibilities to Self: E.2: Diversity. The professional school counselor: (a) affirms the diversity of students, staff and families; (b) expands and develops awareness of his/her own attitudes . . . affecting cultural values . . . and strives to attain cultural competence; (c) possess knowledge and understanding of how oppression, racism. . . . . affects her/him personally and professionally; (d) acquires educational, consultation and training experiences to improve . . . working with diverse populations.

So as we see, our national organization supports our work by giving us guidelines clearly outlining our professional responsibilities around the use of data. Disaggregating data to reveal inequities within the system is directly tied to the ethical standards and thus our work as school counselors. Data can be critically disaggregated to reveal what is or is not happening with a school. For example, disaggregating upper-level math courses by ethnicity or gender could reveal some very interesting information. Does the disaggregated data mirror the overall ethnicity data of the school? If 63% of the school's population is Hispanic and only 19% of the students enrolled in upper-level math classes are Hispanic, what is or is not happening for the Hispanic students?

WHAT DATA IS NEEDED?

Who decides what data is needed? The school counselor? The principal? A parent? A concerned school board member? Of course all of these are stakeholders who will most certainly ask questions about what the data mean, what additional data could be useful, what we can or should do with the data, or how we use the data we have to make effective systemic change.

Our suggestion to you is this: Let the data inform you as to what could potentially be the beginning of the journey. Let's take the math example: low enrollment numbers of Hispanic students in upper-level math in a predominantly Hispanic school. The original data (upper-level enrollment) will open the door for further questions to be asked. But who should ask these questions? Who might be involved in the process?

First and foremost, it is imperative to share the information with your administrator(s) before any further action. Typically the school counselor is involved with students' course selection. And yes, typically, the school counselor knows whether the enrollment patterns are skewed to teachers, time of day, or even course selection. Almost all school counselors instinctively know the reasons for students' course selections—be they good or bad choices, our intuition tells us why such choices are made. But intuition is not enough. We *must* have the hard data clearly articulating what we think we know.

So back to our math problem: we know the math enrollment does not mirror the demographics of the school. What next? It might be prudent to review previous enrollment in lower level math courses to identify demographics. If enrollment of Hispanics in lower level math courses is high and is consistently increasing each year, something is going on!

This additional data would be helpful in outlining your concerns when meeting with your building administrator. You might also have other ideas for further investigation to share with the administrator (a proactive rather than reactive stance). These options could include focus groups with students, conversations with math teachers of both upper and lower courses, and/or a meeting with the entire math department. From this information and data gathering the next step would be to summarize the information and meet again with the building administrator. If the problem looks to be systemic, it might prove prudent to form an inquiry support group (see Chapter 6).

The following list can help you explore potential areas of data. It might prove wise when thinking about these areas for you to also begin to ask yourself how many ways this data might be disaggregated (e.g., ethnicity, gender, time of day) to help shed additional light on your concern.

Data Sources

- Demographics
- School performance (Adequate Yearly Progress; AYP)
- Attainment (making it to or beyond points in the system; e.g., the next grade)
- Achievement (scores or grades, testing, midsemester assessment, homework)
- Opportunity gaps (access to courses; teacher recommendations)
- Test scores
- Enrollment
- Graduation rates
- Attendance
- Discipline
- GPA/class rank
- Retention rates
- Special education
- Dropout rate
- Gender issues
- Learning styles
- Transitions
- Family-school connections to increase academic achievement
- Conflict resolution
- Career tracks
- Work samples
- Referrals
- Sociograms
- Observations
- Journal writing

An excellent source for guiding your inquiry is Ruth S. Johnson's book, *Using Data to Close the Achievement Gap* (2002). Suzanne Klassen (2005) has also created a quick reference guide to using data that might be handy when using Ruth's book for guidance. Choose your data with an eye to what you want to analyze. For instance, GPAs, test scores, graduation rates, and college advancement records can be disaggregated by ethnicity, gender, and SES; grades can be analyzed by department, teacher, or course; and course enrollment can be examined by age, grade level, or teacher.

AVENUES FOR GATHERING DATA

When sources of data are considered, we most often think of disciplinary referrals, failing scores on state assessment tests, or report card grades. Yes, of course these are sources of data. But there are many other venues for gathering data. These include interviews, sociograms, surveys, observations, and audio and/or video recordings.

Interviews (e.g., Focus Groups). Interviews involve orally questioning subjects and recording their responses. The questions might come from a very basic place, or they may be more sophisticated, depending upon the interviewees and your focus of inquiry. Begin by brainstorming questions; then see how well they relate to your topic. Clean and precise questions are essential. They will ensure the same format and questions for each interview or meeting, narrowing the possibilities for the interviewer's subjective inferences. We would caution the interviewer to keep the number of questions to a minimum and to structure each question with language appropriate to the level or age of the individuals to be interviewed. Whenever interviewing students, be knowledgeable about your school district's policies regarding parent permission to talk with a minor. The district might require permission forms signed by *all* parties (see Forms 3.1 and 3.2).

Form 3.1 Sample Informed Consent: Adult Participant

Informed Consent Form

Hello [ADULT'S NAME],

Thank you for considering participation in this project.

Please keep the attached letter detailing the project for yourself. Please sign and return this form to the school counselor [YOUR NAME]. These forms will be held in a confidential location and only the project coordinator, [YOUR NAME], will have access.

I have read the informed consent letter submitted by [YOUR NAME] and I understand that I will be part of a project involving [PROVIDE A BRIEF DESCRIPTION OR TITLE FOR YOUR RESEARCH TOPIC]. I understand the nature of this study and that I can choose to withdraw participation at any time with no penalty.

________ **Yes,** I am willing to participate in this project.

________ **No,** I am not willing to participate in this project.

______________________________ Date: ________________________

Participant's Signature

Form 3.2 Sample Informed Consent Form: Minor Participant

Informed Consent Form

Dear Parent or Guardian,

Please keep the attached letter detailing the project for yourself. Please sign and return this form to your student's classroom teacher/school counselor/school office. These forms will be held in a confidential location and only the project coordinator, [YOUR NAME], will have access.

I have read the informed consent letter submitted by [YOUR NAME] and I understand that my student will be part of a project involving [PROVIDE A BRIEF DESCRIPTION OR TITLE FOR YOUR RESEARCH TOPIC]. I understand the nature of this study and that my student may withdraw from participation at any time with no penalty.

________ **Yes,** I give permission for my student to participate in this project.

________ **No,** I do not give my permission for my student to participate in this project.

______________________________ ______________________________

Student's Name

Student's Signature
[Not necessary, but it is the best practice to include the student's agreement to participate.]

______________________________ Date: ______________________________

Parent's Signature

Using the seventh-grade females failing in math as an example, we could craft questions for our interviews with the failing female students. These questions could be as follows:

1. Describe the materials you come to math class with (books, papers, etc.).
2. Describe how and when you do your homework.
3. Describe what happens when you are in math class.
4. Describe what happens in math class to support your learning.
5. Describe what could better help you learn in math.

Likewise, we could interview the parents of the failing students. Examples of questions to use include the following:

1. When your child talks about math class, what does he or she say?
2. What would help your child succeed in math?
3. What do you see as inhibiting your child's performance in math?

Additionally, information could be gathered from the teacher(s) of the failing students. These questions could be as follows:

1. How do you see student A's work in your class?
2. What would be needed for this student to be successful in math?
3. How would you describe the student's ability in math?
4. What has been done to help the student's performance in class?

The interviews should be recorded on audio or video media for accurate future reference. The recording would also free the interviewer from taking written notes. You will need to address the comfort zone of potential interviewees with either type of recording.

Surveys. Surveys can be a useful tool for gathering information. Questions can be crafted on a Likert scale, as true false, as multiple-choice, as short-answer, on a Semantic Differential scale, or as a ranking task (see Figure 3.1). Before writing the instrument, you must be clear about the information you wish to obtain. If the failing female math students are to be surveyed, what is it you wish to know? Is it about homework completion? How about the atmosphere within the class (e.g., is it inviting)? Or perhaps it might be last

Figure 3.1 Types of Survey Questions

Likert Scale

	Agree Strongly (1)	*Agree (2)*	*Neutral (3)*	*Disagree (4)*	*Disagree Strongly (5)*
The study skills group has helped me feel more confident about my ability to get good grades.					

True False

The study skills group has increased my confidence about getting good grades.	*True*	*False*

Multiple-Choice

The study skills group has had the *most* positive impact on

A. my attendance
B. my grades
C. my confidence
D. none of the above

Short-Answer

How has the study skills group affected your grades?____________________

____

____

Semantic Differential Scale

The goal-setting lesson was

interesting ———————————————————— boring

Ranking

Rank the study skills topics that were most valuable to you from 1 to 6 (1 being most valuable, 6 being least valuable):

_____ Time management
_____ Weekly progress reports
_____ Afterschool tutoring
_____ Goal setting
_____ Stress management
_____ Note taking

year's preparation for this year's course. Was it adequate? Could the same survey be used with parents or teachers?

Sociogram. Preservice preparation for school counselors often includes work with sociograms. Schools are an ideal location for utilizing sociograms. Simply stated, a sociogram is a "picture" of classmates' interactions during an identified time period. A word of caution in the use of sociograms: the information *cannot* be available to anyone other than the data gatherer. Also, the real purpose of the sociogram is to identify social versus isolated individuals. It might be that the failing student happens to be the social director of the class—or, even worse, the class member no one will acknowledge in the attendance.

The sociogram may be generated from observation or from a written questionnaire distributed to the target population (e.g., classes of the seventh-grade female students failing math). Questions are crafted to solicit a response which identifies a specific classmate. For instance, a question could be, If you could work with anyone in the math class, who would it be? Or, Who is good at math? Always remember, the information provided is specific *only* to the math class with only those students in the class. Generalization cannot occur outside the class.

Note Taking. Note taking can take many forms. Whatever the form, note taking can become one of your best resources for guiding your inquiry. Here are some tips and strategies on note taking from Hubbard and Power (2003), modified for school counselors.

Field Notes (FN). Note taking can be any type of notation occurring at any given time. Notes might come from your observations during lunch hour, while students mingle in the halls, at afterschool events, or during class time. The term *field notes* means just that: notes from the field. They are an abbreviated record of what was occurring, nothing more. You will need to set your own system up for note taking. How do you want to categorize and file your notes, as well as record them? Can you do abbreviated note taking and later in the day convert them to a more readable and digestible version on the computer?

As school counselors we don't often think of taking notes in the field. We were trained to write our case notes if needed, but we were never presented with the idea of taking notes while observing students. However, we can learn a great deal from and about our students by sitting back and observing.

Professional Opinion (PO). These notes can be made alongside our note taking. They record what, at that moment, we had as an insight or professional opinion as to what was being observed. For example, I might watch my student during lunch and observe others moving away. I might note: PO = bullying? PO = offensive language? A professional opinion note is just that: a note to remind myself when I review my observations about what my gut was telling me.

My Thoughts (MT). These include side notes about what came to you personally as you were observing and taking notes. Is there another thought or question that arose while you were jotting your notes? Are there other events or circumstances that potentially could be affecting how you are reacting or how the students are interacting? It might be wise to jot down whether you are coming down with the flu or have just received some disturbing personal news. Or maybe something has happened at the school impacting all the students (e.g., fire drill, local award).

Using the template in Figure 3.2, jot down what might be filled in if the failing female math students were to be the focus of your project.

Figure 3.2 Template

Field Notes	*Professional Opinions*	*My Thoughts*

SCHOOL ARTIFACTS

Artifacts. Schools are rich places in which to find and identify already existing data sources. Stepping beyond the everyday data of test scores, attendance, referrals, dropouts, and graduation rates and moving into less thought-of areas of data can provide insights well worth further scrutiny. These areas include master schedules, transcript analysis, school calendars, teacher schedules, student schedules, course syllabi, curriculum content, grading procedures for assignments, and teaching strategies (Crawford & Dougherty, 2003). As Crawford and Dougherty (2003) state, "School artifacts, analyzed with care, offer a gold mine of information about the forces of differentiated expectations that may exist in your schools and classrooms" (p. 28).

Test scores and other hard data can provide the reviewer with concrete numbers and facts regarding student performance, attendance, or graduation. However, to look beyond the hard results and performance data and into the realm of artifacts is a bold move by the educator. Artifacts can help the school look, via a different lens, to what is really happening within the building. With the new information and data the educators can begin to really see and understand what is affecting student achievement. When questions addressed at what is happening in the classes or school to help or hinder teaching and learning are answered through the lens of artifact analysis, administrators, school counselors, and teachers can begin deeper conversations leading to solutions benefiting and supporting all students' high achievement.

Artifact analysis can provide answers to what is happening in the school and in classes prior to the final products of test scores and graduation rates. Artifact analysis provides insightful information about the goings-on within the building. Analyzing how the professionals in the building are utilized during the day, week, and year can provide valuable insight and information. An example of this would be the analysis of monies spent on teachers who deliver the upper-level advanced courses versus those spent on teachers who teach the lower level and regular track courses. In most cases, the analysis bears out the idea that more funding is allocated and spent on advanced courses than on the regular or remedial courses

(Crawford & Dougherty, 2003). Would it better serve ninth- or tenth-grade students to have a seasoned master teacher early in their high school career?

Artifact analysis can guide and inform all stakeholders as they participate in collaborative efforts in school reform. Artifact data is available, needing only to be collected, organized, and analyzed. Deeper questions must be asked when the analysis is brought forward. One question might center around curriculum goals and objectives and whether they are being met. Let's look at one example encountered by a preservice intern.

> Cathy's yearlong internship advocacy project focused on the ninth-grade study skills class, which met daily. Students were identified as being at risk from their eighth-grade report cards (two or more Ds or Fs). The opportunity to voluntarily participate in the class was made to all the identified students. Those students choosing to participate met first hour of each day for the year. The major goals of the class were (1) help students develop quality study skills, (2) develop homework completion skills/strategies, and (3) assist students in achieving passing grades (C or better). Cathy had an intuitive feeling that the class was not increasing students' grades and GPAs. Her project question was: Does participation in the study skills class increase participating students' GPAs when compared with those who elected not to participate?

Why, you might ask, did she ask this question? After being with the class for several weeks, her intuitive feeling was that the original objectives were not being met and the class had become a social gathering place. But she needed hard data! How would you answer her question? How would you gather the data? Would you survey the students? Would you look at the curriculum? Would you administer a pretest and/or posttest of students at the beginning and end of the year? Would you talk with the teachers or parents? Cathy, in partnership with her supervisor and building administrator, elected to examine existing school data (artifacts). She chose the GPAs of students from the previous three years who were offered the opportunity to enroll in the class. She pulled the semester grades of these identified students from their ninth-, tenth-, and eleventh-grade years and compared the two groups (attending versus nonattending). This class had been in effect for four years and was funded on local grant monies. Year four was Cathy's internship year. Cathy's results scared her! After all, she was an intern and had some very startling data to share! Here is what she uncovered: Those students who did *not* participate in the class had higher GPAs over three years than those that had participated in the yearlong class! This data led the teachers and administrators to reconfigure the class and include careful monitoring of the students' classroom performances. Teachers monitored homework completion, quality of completed homework, written work in class, and in-class test scores and provided regular feedback on students' strengths and areas for concerns. The changes in the class were due to Cathy's question.

We have attempted to give you ideas for gathering your data. Sometimes time constraints and the limitations for a given method will be enough to force us to explore a more efficient method. In Table 3.1, you will find a quick chart for your reference when contemplating a given method of gathering your information or data.

THE LAST TIP: HOW TO NAVIGATE DEAD ENDS

So what happens when you are unable to find the data? How can you overcome the obstacles? Begin by starting with the easiest data to collect. It might be your school's demographics or enrollment in ninth-grade algebra classes. By locating this data your confidence in knowing how to navigate the system will increase. Also, doors to other ways of gathering data can potentially be opened for you.

An important note: have your request honed down to a very succinct summary. Leave out the extraneous thoughts or ideas and ask only for the specific piece(s) of data you are trying to locate. Don't be afraid to make the phone call, send the e-mail, or stop by in person. Remember to keep the request simple and clear. For

Table 3.1 Methods for Gathering Information: Pros and Cons

Method	*Pros*	*Cons*
1. Note taking: on-site	More accurate, less reflective, more objective; provides sense of students' experience in a natural setting; allows for contextual considerations.	Takes time away from work with students; very hectic and challenging to capture accurate and comprehensive notes.
2. Note taking: after	More reflective, can be done calmly; allows for learning opportunities to apply to future research; "lessons learned"; may spur new ideas for future projects.	Harder to remember exact transactions or responses after; reflections maybe be influenced by perception of attitude changes over time.
3. Student work	Already part of practice; can provide lots of information for analysis; provides a snapshot of student performance; can show breadth and growth of student skills.	Hard to keep all work and to inform parents; photocopying everything is difficult; storage and organization of work can be time consuming.
4. Interviews	Very valuable information; straight from the horse's mouth; allows for follow-up questions; can be recorded to check for accuracy of data.	Must create time to do this; parental permission required; equipment necessary.
5. Surveys	Another firsthand source of information; not necessary to do frequently; can be used to collect a lot of data from large groups; can ask a variety of questions; can be done anonymously for more honest responses.	Takes time to create a survey if one is not already available; amount and complexity of data may be overwhelming and time consuming; responses may not be specific enough to use.
6. Sociograms	Anytime students work together this is important; can provide information about communication and group dynamics; is focused more on group aspects than on individuals.	Take time; need equipment; harder to intervene on individual level.

7. Audio tapes	Better than notes; can take the place of on-site notes; helps to increase accuracy of data.	Need time to listen and transcribe if needed; sometimes hard to hear; parental permission required.
8. Video tapes	Another lens into your classroom; lots of information; provides a real "face" to the question.	The intrusion factor. Need someone to tape; kids can act differently; who wants to be videotaped; parental permission required; storage issues and confidentiality can be complex.
9. Photos	Capture the moment, good reminder; enhances other data; student motivation.	Need camera and money to develop photos; organization of photos can be time consuming; presentation strategies are critical.
10. Artifacts	Hard evidence; can illustrate the breadth and diversity of data available.	Time consuming; floating; where are they housed?

example, your question might really center on the concern of low Hispanic enrollment in upper-level math courses. When you make the request (via phone, e-mail, or in person), ask for course enrollment in the identified classes to be disaggregated by ethnicity. Don't delve into your subquestions or concerns. Let the data inform you as to "what next."

If you are still running into roadblocks, ask those around you for ideas and suggestions. Again, give them your concerns and questions in a concise format: I'm wondering what the upper-level math course enrollments look like by ethnicity. Period. Let the others brainstorm strategies and ideas for data collection. In all probability, someone will come up with the idea of tracking the numbers from ninth grade to eleventh or twelfth grade. But let them do that—you do not want to influence their brainstorming by inserting your thoughts.

Dianne's Hunch Pays Off

So let's come back to Dianne's journey. She had received the data about the number of third-grade students failing state assessment tests. She knew the teachers were all working very hard to help the students achieve. After visiting with her colleagues and the liaison, Dianne felt as if there was more to the story. Knowing a large percentage of the school's student population was from low-income, single-parent families, Dianne began to look at the larger picture. The test score data had arrived with ethnicity and gender of students. However, Dianne wasn't satisfied with only those pieces of information. She followed her intuition and shared with her principal the test data and what she was thinking. Let's join her in the meeting with her principal with data in hand. This is how she continues her story:

> I thought we should ask for the third-grade test scores to be disaggregated by street addresses—beyond ethnicity and gender. My intuition tells me the majority of the scores will come from one or two of the apartment complexes that continually have problems.

Sharing her ideas with the principal led to a request for disaggregated third-grade test scores by street address. Dianne had followed the recommended steps for investigation by (1) reviewing the data, (2) looking at similar situations and talking with others (e.g., colleagues), (3) stepping back and asking what else might be going on, (4) using her intuitive counseling skills when looking at the specific names of students, and (5) sharing the data and her thoughts with her administrator.

The disaggregated results confirmed her suspicions: the majority of failing students lived in several of the apartment complexes. These complexes had the largest number of students from multiple-sibling, single-parent, low-income families. In addition, the communities within the complexes had long and storied histories of drug use. The data had come back to support her hunch!

In retrospect, it was such a simple question to ask. Have you found yourself in a similar situation? Could you have asked for further clarification or additional data to provide a clearer picture and better understanding of what was going on? Step back and think for a minute about other possibilities that could have been explored? What has Dianne's hunch caused you to think about? Write your thoughts and ideas in Form 3.3 for future reference.

Form 3.3 Free Writing Activity

Free Writing Activity

Multiple Thinking

We need to remind ourselves that we are *better together.* Take your data and share it with your administrators and colleagues. Do your peers have ideas you have missed or forgotten? Ask around. It is more thoughtfully approached when we make it a "we" rather than a "me." Simple. Yet, for whatever reasons, we often find ourselves solving the problem or issue alone or thinking we have the quick fix or answer and need not investigate further.

No matter what data we have, we can always use thoughts and questions from others. Maybe they had a very similar experience that led them to a solution that proved to be in the wrong direction. Without sharing our data and our thoughts, we might never know of their attempts. Additionally, how many of us have thought to ask the students themselves? Could Dianne have talked with individual students or conducted focus groups? Would she have ultimately come to the same conclusion about the two apartment complexes? Or would her conversations have led her in other directions? These are genuine concerns when we begin to think about gathering the supporting data. In Dianne's case, she did consider talking with students. However, because she was familiar with the children and their families, she was able to follow her intuition when she began looking at the data.

What would Dianne have done if the disaggregation had not supported her hunch? We will pursue that in the next chapter when we talk about data analysis.

Sorting It Out 4

Making Sense of Your Data

When a novice school counselor was recently asked about learning to use data, his response was, "I learned that in doing practitioner inquiry work, my job is to put the data on display, allow the data to ask questions, and let the data tell a story." The data analysis step of practitioner inquiry is where the magic happens—where your data unfolds to tell the story, paint the picture, and connect the dots for you and your school community. In this chapter, we will review the many ways to organize, analyze, and conceptualize the data that you have gathered to inform your research. So take this opportunity to learn about the ways that can help you make sense of the data you have uncovered.

DESCRIPTIVE DATA AS A POWERFUL TOOL

Descriptive data provides details about the aspects and extent of any given issue. It does not necessarily require any advanced calculations or fancy statistics, but rather pulls the problem apart and highlights the components that are most relevant to your inquiry. Descriptive data is the foundation of all practitioner inquiry, creating a comprehensive picture that reveals the nature of your research from the start to the finish (Education Trust, 2006). Descriptive data is also powerful because it is compatible with visual presentations. That is, it can be organized in ways that present a visual sense of the work you have accomplished and the meaning of that work. Many audiences respond to a visual presentation of data, whether it is in the form of a graph, diagram, or table. It is important that you consider how to best organize the data once you have analyzed it in order to communicate your research to your intended audience.

WAYS TO LOOK AT DATA

Where do I begin with data analysis? is a common and reasonable question. Our advice is to begin with the simplest analyses and work your way to the more complex. It helps to understand that even the most complex analyses are built on the most simple analyses, so to begin with the basics makes perfect sense. If at that point you want more in-depth or sophisticated information, then keep going. With practitioner inquiry, it is important to keep in mind that there are no hard-and-fast rules about the types of analyses you should use—your decisions depend on the question you are posing and the types of data that will best provide insight into your particular school's issue at hand. In some cases, basic analysis will suffice. In other cases, going beyond the basics will be warranted.

We also recommend that you ask the following questions for each set of data you have gathered:

1. What type of data do I have?
2. How can I best analyze and organize the data?
3. What story does the data tell about my inquiry work?

Step 1. What Type of Data Do I Have?

Many practitioners find that it is most helpful to begin by classifying the available data. Following the guidelines of the American School Counseling Association (2005) *National Model*, there are three types of data: (1) process data, (2) perception data, and (3) results data.

Process data pertains to the process of an event. It is data collected that describe the steps of an activity or details about how an intervention was conducted. It provides facts about the actions you took to track your work. For example, process data may be the brief written description "Eight weekly sessions of a friendship group with six students were held," or "All high school freshman were seen individually to prepare a four-year plan." Process data is the typical type of data collected by working school counselors because it is easy to record and does not require going to many sources to collect; it is usually data already known by the school counselor.

Perception data provides insight into what others think, know, or can demonstrate. Practitioner inquiry research provides an opportunity to gather this type of perception data, which may have been neglected or overlooked before. Assumptions are often made about others' perceptions, but collecting data in this way can provide a platform of factual information for you to actually illustrate the perceptions rather than just assume them. Most perception data measures specific competencies achieved, knowledge gained, or attitudes and beliefs. Examples of competency achievement are that every third-grade student was able to role-play ways to resolve a conflict or that every tenth-grade student completed a career interest inventory. Illustrations of knowledge gained include (1) 92% of first graders can identify an adult at the school to whom they can go for help on the playground, and (2) 87% of teachers correctly listed the primary symptoms of depression in adolescents during an inservice training. Examples of gathering data related to attitudes or beliefs can include (1) 73% of students feel their teachers are supportive or (2) 37% of parents say their child feels safe at school. Often, perception data is collected in the form of a pre- and posttest situation in which a test is given before and after an activity to reveal any changes in thoughts, knowledge, or beliefs via the activity. An evaluation in the form of a survey or competency demonstrations is also a common form of perception data collection.

Results data links the changes to meaningful consequences and effects in your school community. It tells the story of how changes and gains have impacted the objectives of your action research. Results data provides proof of whether or not an activity has positively affected students' ability to use the knowledge, skills, or attitudes to alter their behavior. There is evidence the efforts made did in fact translate to important results. This type of data is more often tied to school improvement plans (SIP). It is less perceptual and based more on firm numbers of behaviors and occurrences. Examples are (1) 82% of students in the study skills group are no longer failing any classes at the end of the term, and (2) fighting incidents have decreased by 25% following completion of the social skills curriculum.

While these types of data can be used independently, it is easy to see that they paint a more colorful picture, and make more sense to the audience, when all types are represented and recognized accordingly. Knowing which type of data you have collected can help you make clear connections to your original research question and can also provide details of your entire study at all stages.

Step 2. How Can I Best Analyze and Organize the Data?

Basic Analyses

The best way to analyze the data you have is to start with simple statistics, primarily averages and percentages. These simple yet effective analyses provide important information that help describe the current situation. These analyses are also easy for educators and the general public to understand and read. In fact, your audience may respond best to basic analyses rather than sophisticated and complex strategies for describing your data.

Using averages and percentages to analyze your data is also a good approach when you are describing the population of your entire school or district. When your entire student or staff population is the reference group, using averages or percentages can provide a contextual snapshot of the issue. For example, Anytown Elementary School has an enrollment of 540 students in Grades K–5. Last year, 83% of our students passed the math benchmark test and 63% passed the English/language arts benchmark test (see Figure 4.1).

These basic analyses are also useful when comparing pre- and posttest data. It is an easy way to read the results at each point in time and consider whether or not the changes are related to an implemented intervention or change.

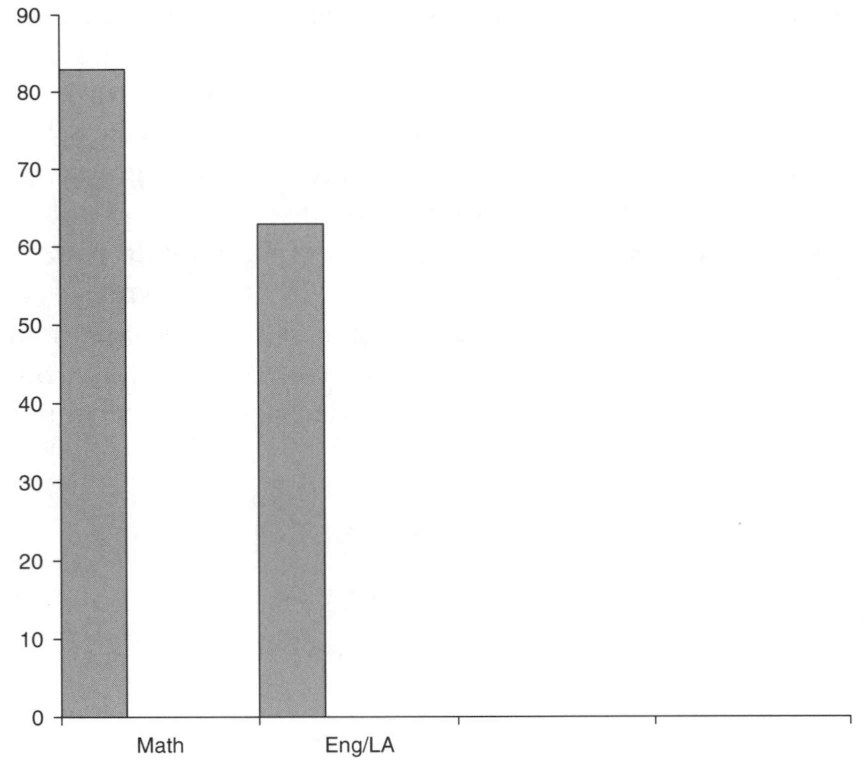

Figure 4.1 Number of Students Who Passed the Math and English/Language Arts Benchmark Tests

Longitudinal Data Analysis

To provide a more comprehensive picture using averages and percentages, consider using a longitudinal approach to your data. Longitudinal data are collected over time using the same target population. Longitudinal data can inform the audience of any long-term patterns or trends and provide a relative sense of gains and losses (Education Trust, 2006). They may also spur discussion about the contextual factors (e.g., the adoption of new curriculum, the implementation of a new intervention, the addition of new staff) that may have contributed to the changes over time specific to your school community.

Have you ever wondered how your school has performed on a particular set of data over several years or wanted to compare a particular behavior or performance over time? Are you wondering if your current research topic is a "new" concern for your school and students? Maybe you are interested in detecting increases, decreases, or stability of certain indicators over time in your school? In these cases, longitudinal data, if available, would be a great choice for analyzing and presenting your data.

For example, let's take the sample used above and report it as longitudinal data. We can still use averages and percentages, but present the data from several years. Figure 4.2 shows longitudinal data on the percentage of students at Anytown Elementary School who have passed the math and English/language arts benchmark test over the last four years.

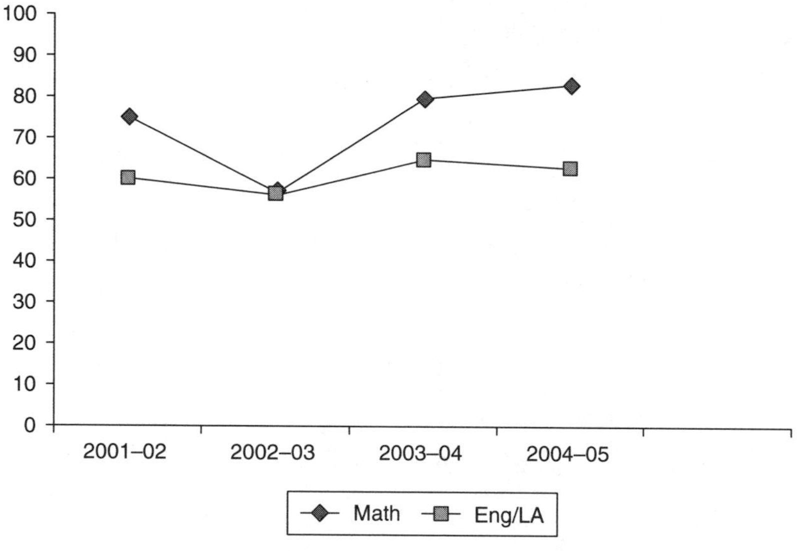

Figure 4.2 Percentage of Students Who Passed the Math and English/Language Arts Benchmark Test (2001–2005)

Disaggregated Data Analysis

Another approach to analyzing data is to disaggregate data by categories. To disaggregate data is to "subdivide performance data by any categories we suspect could be relevant" (Sagor, 2005, p. 122). It allows the researcher to look more closely at the details of the data to determine where the discrepancies are within the larger group and where the work should be focused.

Disaggregated data has been promoted in recent publications in the field of school counseling as a powerful tool for identifying inequities in educational practices. Disaggregating data is the most helpful approach when trying to identify factors that may contribute to differences among student performance, attitudes, or knowledge within your school. Basic averages and percentages may miss an important part of the story and simplify a very complex issue. On the other hand, disaggregated data can point to access and equity issues and highlight which groups of students are underserved and in need of additional attention. While disaggregated data may help us understand more specifically the experience of some student groups, Johnson (2002) also urges educators to avoid lumping students together by examining within-group differences that will go beyond initial assumptions.

So what are the various ways that data can be disaggregated? What are the typical categories that we want to look at more closely? How are our data compiled, and how can we break our data down further to understand the intricacies of the situation? Table 4.1 provides a reference for disaggregating your data.

These are some major categories that might guide data disaggregation. While this is not an exhaustive list, the categories are typical and feasible ways of disaggregating data that are common to school counselors' practice. You can begin to see how looking at data in different ways can lead to various insights. For example, you will elicit different information if you disaggregate special education by ethnicity; perhaps you will discover that 80% of special education students are African American. Or disaggregating dropout rates by gender may reveal that 75% of dropouts are male. You may also uncover data that illuminate positive circumstances in your school, such as that 50% of ethnic minority students are enrolled in AP courses when the ethnic minority student population makes up less than 50% of your total school population.

In this table, it is also important to notice that the same data point can be disaggregated using different definitions. That is, disaggregating graduation rates can be calculated in more than one way. The definition of *graduation rate* may differ from school to school,

Table 4.1 Examples of Data Points to Examine

Data Category	*Specific Areas*
Test scores	Achievement
	State
	National
Enrollment	Honors/AP classes
	College track
	Special education
	LEP[a]
Graduation rate	By gender
	By ethnicity
	By SES[b]
Attendance	Absences
	Tardies
	By grade level
Discipline	By classroom
	Types of problems
	Gender
GPA/Class rank	By gender
	By ethnicity
	By SES
Retention rates	By subject area
	By grade level
	By gender, ethnicity
	Postsecondary
	Plans
Special education	By gender
	By ethnicity
	By SES
Dropout rate	Grade levels
	Gender, ethnicity
	Reasons why

Source: Reprinted from Education Trust (2006).

a. LEP = limited English proficiency.
b. SES = socioeconomic status.

so it is vital that you explicitly predetermine the definition of graduation rates for your school in your data analysis. Will the graduation rates data point be determined by the number of students who do not receive a diploma, or will it be determined by the number of students who entered as ninth-graders and exit as graduates? Do you then disaggregate graduation rates by gender, ethnicity, and socioeconomic status? As you can see from this example, there is no right or wrong way to make these determinations. Instead it is critical that you define these data points clearly during the explanation of your disaggregated data.

Interview, Observation, and Narrative Analysis

There are particular ways to analyze qualitative data, including interview, observation, and narrative analysis. The first place to start in analyzing this data is to develop written or typed transcriptions (from a videotape, an audiotape, or original notes) that account for *all* the data you have from these sources. Every bit of information elicited from the source should be included in this account. After you have carefully read the written transcriptions, often several times, consistent themes and patterns should emerge. Ask yourself, What are the topics that keep arising throughout the data? Are there distinct points that several people have mentioned that seem to be repeated over and over? Themes may range from broad categories to very detailed points, depending on your interest. You will want to define and describe these themes as thoroughly as you can from the start, which is often a transitory process. That is, your themes may evolve as you go through your data, thereby allowing your themes to be informed by the data you gathered.

Analyzing Themes. Developing a list of these themes and the corresponding data from the original transcriptions is the next step. There are several ways to do this, but for working school counselors who are constrained by real-world demands on the amount of time, availability, and resources they have to dedicate to research, the basic ways of analyzing data are the most realistic. You may want to use large pieces of chart paper to create a visual picture of each thematic category and the supporting data under each heading. You may want to place each data point on a 3×5 card and shuffle the cards under various categories until you find the right fit. You may want to place all the written data on your computer and cut and paste different points under the most fitting categories. Whichever strategy seems to work best for your data and your learning style should be your initial approach.

Another important step in this process will require help from members of your practitioner inquiry team. To ensure that you are acting as objectively as possible and to lend more credibility to your choices for themes, you will want another team member to review and provide feedback about your analysis. Another pair of eyes on the data will help you answer questions you may have or present new ideas for themes that you may not have noticed on your own. This is a fundamental way of increasing reliability and validity in your practitioner inquiry project and is often a stimulating and exciting part of your work as you and your team see the data coming together.

Once this is done, and you have analyzed your data according to thematic categories, you can present the data by creating a table that includes your themes or codes and includes snippets of data from the transcriptions that support each theme. Presenting your data in this manner is clear and engaging to the audience because you are taking authentic data, direct from the original responses, and organizing it in a way that informs your practitioner inquiry question.

Coding

For observations, in particular, you may want to develop a coding system. Codes are usually devised to record particular behaviors, interactions, or other dynamics that are defined prior to the actual observation. Observation codes can range from very simple to very complicated, so your research question and the amount of detail that you want from your data will determine the level of complexity for your codes. These codes then guide the recordings made during the observation: They are a type of shorthand used to record what is being observed. After the observation has been completed and the codes have been recorded, you will want to thoroughly review the frequency and nature of each code occurrence. It is imperative that you have others check your work here, just as with the theme analysis, to verify that your codings are valid and reliable. Once agreements and discussions with your team members have taken place, you can then compile a list of the frequencies per code category, along with any other supportive information from the observations. Your list will capture the patterns within your coded data and allow you to bring them to light when you present your research to an audience.

Meta-Analysis

One of the most important but often neglected strategies for data analysis is the process of meta-analysis: paying attention to your own practitioner inquiry experience. As a reflective practitioner, you may be doing this in several aspects of your job already. In terms of practitioner inquiry, there are several ways to document your thoughts and ideas as you pursue your research and involve yourself in the process. Common strategies include writing reflective field notes, maintaining a personal journal, compiling notes from consulting situations regarding your project, and saving artifacts from your research experience. You may want to keep anecdotes, artifacts, or pictures that capture the "faces" of your inquiry to help bring your work to life. In addition to your own reflections, you will want to gather data in the form of peer input and colleagues' feedback, as described in Table 4.2.

Table 4.2 Suggestions for Peer Input and Feedback

Discuss the following with colleagues who were involved in your practitioner inquiry project or observed you during the inquiry process:

- Ideas for project improvement
- Recognition of successful strategies
- Problem-solving ideas for challenging or difficult issues encountered
- Organizing tasks and deadlines
- Strategies to increase cooperation among key stakeholders
- Recommendations for collecting or analyzing data
- Presentation run-throughs prior to a final presentation

Your personal experiences during the practitioner inquiry process are valuable! Using your reflections to inform your future research planning, or to help support a colleague in his or her pursuits, is an excellent idea. The data may point you toward ways to avoid mistakes, create shortcuts, or document the decisions you made during your inquiry experience. You may have some very specific ideas from your reflections (e.g., "Permission slips took longer to return, needed to send them out earlier," or "Ms. Montaño has some expertise in this area, ask for her help next time") or more general ideas (e.g., "Maybe apply for a grant to keep this program going," or "Expand to include more females next time"). Based on the amount and quality of your meta-analysis data, you may be amazed at how much you learned during your inquiry process and how much you have to offer as you continue to develop professional inquiry skills.

The meta-analysis process can also help to identify areas of bias that may have impacted your practitioner inquiry project. Bias is inherent in all research, thus the goal is to reduce bias by becoming aware of it and taking steps to address it. During your reflective meta-analysis, you will want to ask yourself the following questions to recognize potential bias:

- What are your expectations for this project?
- Who is represented in the study and who is not?
- Whom did you seek guidance from while formulating your project?
- What philosophical foundations and assumptions about education did you rely on during your project?
- What do you know about the practitioner inquiry topic already that is impacting your perspective and guiding your project?
- What are the answers you are looking for even before you analyze the data?
- In terms of organization and planning, what worked to gather the most telling data?

Reflecting on these questions may shed light on some of the influences that you were not aware of otherwise. You may realize that some of these biases had an unintentional impact on your work, which you will want to share during your presentation and also consider while planning your future projects.

Step 3. What Story Does the Data Tell About My Practitioner Inquiry Question?

Now that you have taken steps to analyze your data, you will want to put together the entire story in relation to your practitioner inquiry question and objectives. For an example of dropout data at Yourtown High School, see Figure 4.3.

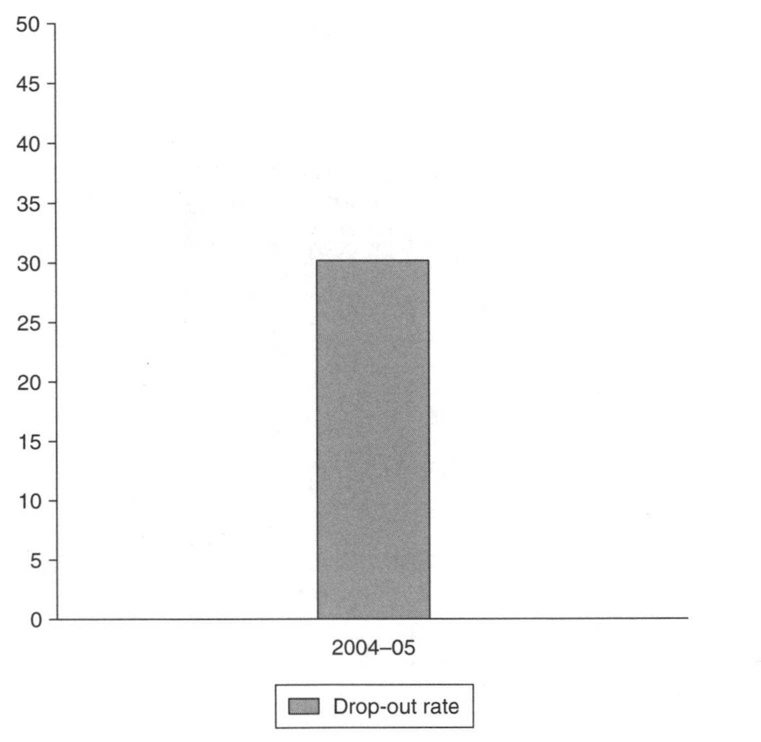

Figure 4.3 Dropout Rate for Yourtown High School (2004–2005)

What does this data tell you? What doesn't this data tell you? At first glance, it tells a story of dropout rates at Yourtown High School. Any dropout rate, no matter how high or low, will be a concern to the school. It conveys that there is a group of students who are not achieving the graduation goal of the school. What it doesn't explain is what is going on in the school environment that may be influencing the data (Education Trust, 2006). It tells only part of the story. What other data may you want to request to more fully tell the story?

Perhaps you want to examine differences across ethnic groups, so the data is disaggregated by ethnicity (see Figure 4.4).

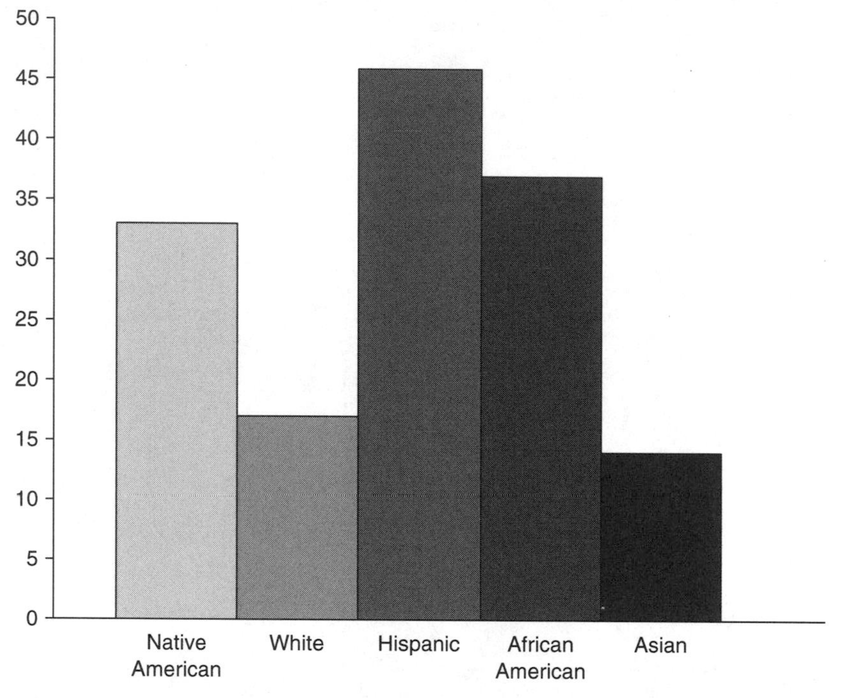

Figure 4.4 Dropout Rate for Yourtown High School Disaggregated by Ethnicity

The disparities become clear when you disaggregate the data by ethnicity. The data tell a story of opportunity or service gaps that may factor into those data. If the dropout rates are much higher for students of color when compared to the building demographics, this is evidence of a problem in need of systemwide attention. With intervention is changes in opportunity and access, the data, when revisited, will hopefully tell a different story.

Disaggregating data is an opportunity to explore beyond the initial set of data. In an attempt to remain alert to the hidden surprises of your data's story, it is imperative that you follow the ideas arising from the disaggregated data rather than holding on to only your initial ideas. Educator Victoria Bernhardt states, "Disaggregation is not a problem-solving strategy. It is a problem-finding strategy" (Victoria Bernhardt as cited in Education Trust, 2006, Module 1 Slide 50). This philosophy encourages you to listen carefully and diligently to the story that unfolds as your data are analyzed.

Let's go beyond disaggregation and move toward examining new data. Perhaps as part of an attempt to address the dropout rate at Yourtown High School, the school counselor gathered additional data on reasons that students cite when considering dropping out (see Table 4.3).

The data reveals that students perceive that school is boring,

Table 4.3 Students' Reasons for Dropping Out

Reason Cited	*Percentage Citing (N = 97)*
School was boring	76
I don't feel that I belong here	68
I was not learning enough	42

they experience a sense of disconnection to the school, and they are not learning. What is going on in school for students to say this? The school is apparently engaging other students, those who are graduating, enough for them to stay. What are these students not receiving so that they are feeling disenfranchised from school? The answers to these questions are opportunity gaps. What are possible systemic activities that could be implemented to address this data? These questions are guiding your story. Pursue each question with an open mind and persistent awareness.

In these examples, several steps were taken to interpret the data and tell the story. With each set of data, you are looking for patterns, suggestions, and gaps. Closely examine the data for "holes" in the data and specific areas of concern. Questions to guide you in the critical analysis phase of [illegible]king with the data include, What problems or needs surfa[illegible] at achievement gaps exist? What opportunity gaps do th[illegible] suggest? What are the systemic contributions to the pro[illegible] The story will naturally lead to solutions and ideas for syste[illegible]hange in your school.

Uncovering Opportunity Gaps

Using data as a tool to uncover opportunity gaps in student populations has been the focus of several recent publications (Bauman, 2004; Brown & Trusty, 2005; Stone & Dahir, 2004; Johnson, 2002; Rowell, 2005; Rowell, 2006; Sink, 2006; Whiston, 2002). Data has the power to demonstrate the nature and extent of problems in our schools. Data can substantiate the need to address a problem (e.g., Hey! Look over here! This is a big problem!) so that all students and the entire school environment benefit. It also has the power to highlight what we are doing well and how we are meeting the needs of students. A primary role of school counselors, both professionally and ethically, is to continuously monitor and address inequities in our schools. Our purpose is to ask the difficult questions and point out the discrepancies that impact the students who are most in need of services. Using data to do this in big and small ways is our responsibility.

One question to ask yourself is, What do I know about educational equity? For some, equity is recognizing that not all students start the school experience, or the school year, with the same opportunities, background, and histories. It is about being willing to make special considerations for individual students and for groups of students in our schools in order to accomplish schoolwide goals for all students. To begin this mission, we ask questions and explore the data with this sense of equity in mind.

We can look for inequities in our school practices by comparing opportunities and student performance with the demographics of the school. Gauging whether or not students are represented at adequate rates is an imperative task. There are several categories to review when examining equity practices in our schools (Education Trust, 2006):

Student Demographics: What are the characteristics of our students and staff?

- Gender
- Ethnicity
- Socioeconomic status (participation in free/reduced lunch program)

- English proficiency level
- Family configuration
- Mobility
- Percentage and distribution of highly qualified teachers in school (Slide 33)

Student Attainment: How many students make it to, and beyond, key points in the school system?

- Advancement to the next grade
- Graduation rate
- Transition from middle school to high school/feeder schools
- Type of high school diploma
- Meeting additional graduation requirements: portfolios, projects, exit exams
- Matriculation to an institution of higher education
- Earning a college degree (Slide 39)

Student Achievement: What does achievement look like at different levels and with different groups of students?

- Overall achievement
  - Grade point average
  - Standardized test scores
  - Passing all subjects
- Periodic assessment
  - Semester grades
  - End of course tests
- Ongoing classroom assessment
  - Class assignment grades
  - Tests (Slide 35)

Student Behavior Choices: What are students doing?

- Attendance
- Discipline referrals
- Classroom behavior
- Homework completion

- Enrollment patterns
  - Pre-algebra in eighth grade
  - Algebra in ninth grade
  - Electives in middle and high schools
  - Upper-level math and science
  - Honors, AP, college credit (Slide 37)

Student Opportunity Gaps: Are some students provided more opportunities than others?

- Access to rigorous curriculum
- Access to quality teachers
- School policies and climate
- Special education screening and placement
- Participation in support services such as tutoring, mentoring, and study skills groups (Slide 41)

Student Possibilities: Are there schools that show things could be different? Find schools that look like yours and have done one or more of the following:

- Closed the opportunity gaps
- Closed the achievement gap
- Developed innovative and feasible interventions or programs (Slide 42)

If you are looking at achievement or attainment data and find concerns in these areas, don't stop there. Start to look for the opportunity gaps that may be behind the data. There may be situations in which some students receive the support and resources they need to be successful in school while the support and resource needs of other students are not met. Some students have computers (for Internet access and word processing) at home while others don't. Some students have relationships with adults at school who believe in their potential; many students do not have a mentor-type relationship with any adult at school. Unfortunately, opportunity gaps abound, and the real solutions to address equity are inherent there.

- If students of color are underrepresented in upper-level courses, what made that happen? Do faculty members believe that all students need to enroll in rigorous courses? Does the school staff understand the doors that automatically close for these students if they do not take the rigorous courses? Do the students themselves believe that this is important? Are systemic barriers in place (e.g., prerequisite classes or teacher recommendation) that are potential roadblocks for enrollment?
- If subgroups of students are not achieving at the same level as their peers, what support services do the subgroups need in order to help close the achievement gap? For example, do some students need additional time spent in reading instruction?
- Do some students need access to additional resources? We have already mentioned the importance of looking at teacher assignments, adult mentors, and academic support services.
- When looking at data, always check out how opportunity gaps may be contributing to achievement gaps (Education Trust, 2006).

Many school counselors ask, What should be our goal? How will we know when we have achieved educational equity in our practices? One strategy is to set goals so that representation is achieved that mirrors the demographics of your school. For example, if you have a student population that is 53% male, but only 23% of the AP English course is male, then there is an underrepresentation of males in that college preparatory course. Thus the goal would be to increase the male enrollment in the course to match the general student population. This often leads to questions about making systemic changes at the expense of students already enrolled. The fact is that identifying the inequities *should* lead to changes, changes that may be unprecedented and have far-reaching consequences on schedules, staff responsibilities, and the status quo. But adding courses, increasing student participation, and positioning students for lifelong advantages will require thinking outside of the box.

Another strategy is to set a goal of a particular percentage gain. Perhaps you want to increase the number of students of color taking college entrance tests in your school, and you determine that a 20%

increase is realistic. In setting a new goal for your school, it is important to discuss the possibilities with your advisory team and administration so that you can collectively agree on a feasible yet constructive goal. Additionally, your School Improvement Plan (SIP) and District Improvement Plan (DIP) can have considerable influence in your identification of particular goals.

While the ideas of mirroring demographics and setting sensible goals are important, it is also critical to consider that these rates should not be the optimum goal. Instead, they are the minimum goal, and as educators we should strive to improve practices for *all* students. While achieving matching percentages may be the initial goal, the ultimate goal should be to exceed the minimum and eventually reach 100% of students. It is this belief in educational equity that should guide our inquiry work.

School counselors are poised with the knowledge and resources to spur the actions that lead to educational equity. Using data to practice continuous inquiry and monitor student opportunities and performance is the basis for equity work. Gathering information about your school and district environment can provide insight into factors otherwise unconsidered. Assessing the progress of all students should be a foremost goal. Monitoring the outcomes and effectiveness of programs, policies, and practices helps to understand the impact of the system on individual students and groups of students. And last, it is in everyone's best interest that problem solving is based on accurate information that tells a truthful and factual story. Data informs the audience of your story, activates a process toward solutions, and tells a tale of educational equity.

Dianne Makes Sense of It All

Dianne began making sense of her yearly test score data by first looking at the information provided: student name, ethnicity, gender, grade, and test scores. Remember Dianne visited with colleagues about the failing students and what was potentially contributing to their failure. After visiting with her colleagues, Dianne stepped back and away from the data. She used the information she had garnered from colleagues and the principal. She knew she was on track by asking for the data to be further disaggregated by street addresses. We call this "peeling the onion"—pulling one layer off at a time to reveal what is beneath. The street address data gave Dianne and the team valuable information.

Now the team knew where the largest number of failing students lived: several apartment complexes. Armed with this information, they were able to begin deeper conversations regarding intervention possibilities. Earlier Dianne had strategized with the liaison to the Community Partnerships for Affordable Housing. The team pondered what to do next. Do we try talking to the apartment complexes first? Do we engage other members of the school and/or community? Are there others we have forgotten or do not know about?

The street address data seems to clearly point to the next step: a brainstorming session with the stakeholders. Excitement filled the room. Concerned and committed parties would be coming together to discuss strategies for helping all students achieve to high standards.

What would have happened if the disaggregated street address data had not supported Dianne's hunch? What would you have done? Where would the data have taken you or Dianne? No one knows. But we can be sure of this: the groundwork that Dianne and the team did would have ensured that, regardless of the disaggregated data outcome, strategies for helping the students would have been the focus of conversations. And we can also be assured that the data would have been central in the conversations. When we use data to guide our work, we find that it can and will enlighten our paths to use the right strategies at the right time.

Stepping Up 5

Sharing What You Now Know

It is time to share all that you have learned during your practitioner inquiry journey! This is an opportunity for you to tell your entire story, describe the details and impact of your work, and leave your audience with lasting impressions. In this chapter, we will take a look at the different avenues for communicating your work, strategies for working efficiently and creatively, and important details to incorporate as you step up and share with others what you now know.

THE FUNDAMENTALS

There are a few fundamental ways to share your work. The first is to write about it. Writing up your work may take the form of a report that is professionally written and documents the procedures and outcomes of your work with some brevity. Reports are typically written in a straightforward and understated manner that provides an account of events, which may not allow for much ingenuity or many reflective ideas. Sometimes reports will be required for your practitioner inquiry project, especially if there is funding or project management involved. In these cases, there are usually guidelines about the sections and content required in the report. Reports are often regarded as a way of summarizing and documenting your work, not necessarily for publicizing the amazing, or just plain positive, elements of your efforts. However, reports are helpful for providing a concise, direct, and relevant write-up of your inquiry work. For some educators, a report may be the preferred choice for the write-up because it is structured and succinct.

You may be asked to write a more detailed paper as a means of communicating your work. For graduate students or recent graduates, the expectation of a written paper is probably familiar. For practicing school counselors, it may feel more like a lofty request, but writing up your work in the form of a paper can be an extremely helpful and pleasant process. Papers allow for flexibility in your writing and organization; they let you present your work from your own perspective while basing your conclusions in facts and information. In any given circumstance, the expectations for the paper may be different. For example, in one situation, the paper should be professionally written with particular headings and details and with limited subjective aspects. In another situation, the paper might be written in casual language and include subjective points made throughout in an effort to illustrate the authenticity and influence of the work. When it comes to writing a paper, be sure to identify the purpose and the best writing style for your particular case. This will allow you to make the best choices as you get ready to compose your paper.

Writing an article for a professional journal, magazine, Web site, or other publication is another option. There is a lot of variability when it comes to writing for the types of professional publications that may involve input from publishers, editorial boards, or reviewers. If you are interested in pursuing an article, take some time to review the actual publication where you hope to submit your writing and review any guidelines or procedures for that particular publication. Some publications have periodic "calls for papers"; others have ongoing solicitations and submission opportunities. It is important to realize that writing an article for a professional publication can be a lengthy process that has several phases of submission, review, editing, and publishing. Online journals may involve a speedier process because the avenues may not be as standardized or extensive as for traditional journals. Magazines often look for brief, interesting, reader-friendly writings that will appeal to their respective audiences. Again, looking into the various sites, opportunities, and requirements for the publication that piques your interest is going to be the most helpful starting point.

Summarizing your work in a brochure or flyer is an efficient and interesting way to share your inquiry project. This approach provides an appealing snapshot of your project and may include an overview as well as details of your work. Actual data samples, such as charts, graphs, or tables, are highly conducive to brochures or flyers, as they attract the eye amidst the written text. There are templates available from word processing software that provide the structure for creating brochures and flyers; you need only input the information. Distribution is also less complicated, as you can imagine reaching more people with a simple one-page description of your work than with a lengthy paper. Brochures and flyers are a good choice in situations where you want to communicate your work to many people in your immediate community, not necessarily to reach professional audiences on a large scale.

A second fundamental approach to sharing your work is through a live presentation. A presentation may be your attempt to personally reach your school community, other educators or professionals, or current or potential stakeholders (such as community organizations, institutions of higher education, or funding organizations). Presentations allow you to act in the role of the storyteller as your project unfolds with a live audience. This approach is an opportunity for a more dynamic, interactive, and creative mode of communication compared to a written document.

As with a written approach, you have many choices when it comes to developing a presentation. A presentation can be organized according to your preferences and available resources. The way that you decide to frame your story, provide details, and explain the impact of your work is up to you. Presenting your work to a live audience will require that you are a comfortable and engaging speaker on some level, or that you select someone involved in the work to present who is comfortable and engaging. Whether it is fair or not, a presenter's speaking talent can make a huge difference in the audience's perception of the quality of the work being presented, so carefully considering your skills in this area is an essential step.

Your available resources, particularly technological resources, may also influence the elements of your presentation. Some educators are a whiz with technology, able to whip up a colorful, lively, highly professional presentation with all of the video and animation bells and whistles. Others are still mastering the basics of word processing and using overheads. And yet others may be confined by the technology available in their schools, even if they have the skills and knowledge to utilize more advanced tools. There is no standard when it comes to incorporating technology in presentations, but if you are able or interested in using it, then by all means, go for it. You may want to have a visual to help guide your audience through your main points while you speak. Or you may want to highlight particular data by presenting graphs or charts for all to see. You might use posters, overhead transparencies, or computer programs to develop these ideas. Some popular choices include using Microsoft PowerPoint templates, scanning or importing photographs, or streaming digital video into the presentation. You may also consider building a Web site (or having someone build one for you) that publicizes your work. Perhaps developing a video for distribution is an ambitious but exciting idea. And remember that while fancy technology may make a presentation seem more appealing, the bottom line is that this is about presenting your work. The content will be more important than the presentation every time.

There may be new and creative ideas for sharing your work already present in your school environment. You may know of an innovative method of sharing work with colleagues that was developed from your specific school culture. Maybe your school leaders have ideas for preferred ways of highlighting efforts of staff members. Maybe several staff members have undergone training in an organizational model that encourages communication using specific strategies. New technology is emerging that may spark fresh ideas. Keep your eyes and ears open for ways of conveying your work that you may not have discovered before.

For additional suggestions about developing quality writings and presentations, read on.

KNOW YOUR AUDIENCE

It is critical to consider who will make up the audience when you share your work. Your audience will determine various aspects of your presentation, whether it is a written document or a live presentation. Some potential audiences may be school administrators, school staff, students, parents, school board members, community members, community agencies or organizations, funding organizations, or colleagues attending a professional conference. You may also have a mixed audience full of members from all the groups listed, with different interests and expectations for learning about your work. While you cannot account for everyone who may be reading or hearing about your inquiry work, you can plan by asking yourself the following questions:

Language: What type of language will my audience appreciate? Is it an audience that prefers that I write or speak professionally, using jargon and terms that I can assume they are familiar with already? Or is this an audience of laypeople or community members who prefer a more casual approach?

Role as an Expert: Does my audience prefer that I communicate as an expert or that I defer to their added expertise instead?

Background Knowledge: Does my audience have a background or experience in the topic at hand, or would they appreciate that I set a foundation for my work and start with the basics?

Length: Will my audience expect to read or hear a lengthy description of my work or perhaps get in-depth coverage of the most relevant details, or are they anticipating a brief overview only?

Facilities: Particularly for a live presentation, where will it be taking place? Who has access and transportation to reach the site? Who will feel most comfortable in the surroundings? How will I feel in this environment?

KNOW YOUR END PRODUCT

As you think about your practitioner inquiry work, what are some of the most meaningful aspects of it? If you could communicate only a few points, which would be the most significant to convey? Reflecting on the aspects of your work that you *really* want to communicate will help ground your ideas as you share them. Knowing what you want to tell others will help to organize yourself and keep you from deviating from your objectives. If you find that your writing or presentation is getting too lengthy, or if you have limited opportunity to share your work, then refer back to your major points to keep you focused.

Think about your primary goal for the work. Was it to increase awareness within your own school community? Was it to provide evidence of your efforts to the school board? Was it to share new ideas with other professional colleagues and educators? Was it to illustrate to students their own gains and successes? Your goals and purposes will help to clarify the main messages that you want to get across as you share your work.

INQUIRY SUPPORT GROUPS

Joining a group of fellow researchers within your school or district can be very helpful. These group members might lend a hand as you strive to stay motivated, to keep things in perspective, and to stay accountable for moving forward with your project. You may also be surprised by how much you learn when you support colleagues through their projects.

Such groups can be structured in various ways. Perhaps it is a group that meets monthly to discuss each others' project progress. Maybe you schedule it as you go according to availability. Perhaps you develop a timeline of tasks and hold each other accountable for bringing pieces of work to the group for discussion. Maybe it is a brainstorming group that solves problems encountered during the inquiry process. If a support group does not exist, then consider establishing a group. Sometimes even having one colleague who is invested in the quality of your inquiry work can be a great help. The old adage is "two heads are better than one." When it comes to practitioner inquiry, having a supportive colleague (or several) and a thoughtful sounding board can be a wonderful advantage.

ROUTINES

Most people need some structure to complete a task such as developing a written document or spoken presentation of their work. This is a sizeable undertaking, and setting up an environment that will facilitate productivity is crucial. Take some time to take inventory of your personal style when it comes to accomplishing tasks. Identify your learning style by reflecting on how you best integrate and retain information. There are several theories that provide descriptors for personal learning styles and multiple intelligences (Armstrong, 1994; Dunn & Stevenson, 1997; Gardner, 2006). Do you connect to material best when it is presented in a visual, auditory, or tactile manner? Do you prefer to interact with material as you learn or follow more traditional didactic strategies? In terms of organizational style, what are your best practices? Do you prefer to write lists, create timelines, use a filing system, put materials in piles, or figure it out as you go? If you don't think of yourself as an organized person, this is the time to change that! Even the most basic steps can be taken, such as designating a particular spot where you direct all papers for your project or designating some amount of time every week to spend on your project.

Take the time to consider the importance of a productive space that works for you. Keep in mind that "productive" does not necessarily mean quiet and secluded. For some, this is ideal and may be the best setting for getting those tasks completed. But let's face it, for working school counselors, you just want to identify a place that will work well enough for you to concentrate, deal with minimal interruptions, and house the resources you need to accomplish your project. Having a designated spot will help you to feel organized and prepared to work when the opportunity arises.

THE BLOCK

For every practitioner, there will likely be moments when you are stuck, blocked, or bored with the practitioner inquiry project that you have undertaken. Those moments of staring at the computer screen or racking your brain for that one elusive idea can be agonizing. While this may be normal, it is still a difficult situation that calls for a kick-start.

One strategy is to concentrate on baby steps instead of lofty goals. Can you break down the task so that you are still moving forward, even if it is not at the pace you wished? Are there preliminary steps you could take that might make your work easier in the end? It may also help to work on another aspect of the project, then go back when the time is better. For others, taking a break altogether is the best strategy. Taking yourself out of the pressure and spending your time on enjoyable activities may actually energize you to get back to work with a more positive and inspired attitude.

Speaking as counselors, of course, we cannot ignore the importance of environmental issues that may be impacting your work. It may be that stress or anxiety in other aspects of your life are affecting your ability to concentrate on your project. Perhaps there are professional pressures attached to this project that feel burdensome. It is important that you take steps to manage the stress and prioritize your personal needs in relation to your work-related commitments.

If you are encountering "inquiry block," find time to relax. Don't make more demands of yourself; instead be open to letting inspiration hit you wherever you may be. Keep a notepad handy for those unexpected moments when the light bulb turns on. Sometimes it just takes one good idea to get the ball rolling, and after that you want to be prepared for the outpouring that follows.

When we encounter stagnation, it may indicate a lack of interest or motivation in the project. Some projects can lose their appeal over time and it is important that we maintain a sense of investment and purpose in what we do. Find *something* that motivates you. Talk to students who look to you as a problem solver. Reflect on positive aspects of your job and the difference that you make for your school community. Think about your value for ongoing professional development and your ability to accomplish new and challenging responsibilities. All educators have their own motivation for doing the work they do, and this may be your opportunity to reclaim your own motivation.

DEADLINES

For some people, deadlines are a cruel fact of life, and for others they are a blessing in disguise. Perhaps you adhere to deadlines imposed by others or hold yourself to your own standards of time limits. Do deadlines tend to help you or hurt you?

If deadlines are a part of your work life, then take some time to explore your personal responses to and attitude about deadlines. In your experience, how did you feel when you didn't meet a deadline? When you did meet a deadline? What emotional responses were related to that experience (e.g., glee, satisfaction, anxiety, distraction)? In this situation, when you are working on telling others about your project, would deadlines push you forward or just create more stress?

If instilling some form of deadline or schedule is a strategy that works for you, consider these ideas. For some people, working backward and creating deadlines from the eventual goal works well. If you have an end point that you want to reach, identify the steps and time points you want to accomplish between the beginning and the end, and hold yourself accountable to those deadlines. Another strategy is to create and abide by a calendar that illustrates your project goals. This is less structured than a deadline schedule, but provides a sense of tasks to do in the context of the big picture. Placing the calendar in a prominent place will remind you as the days pass. A calendar gives you some leeway because the calendar dates are not necessarily hard deadlines, but hopeful targets. It is also helpful to anticipate a plan for solving problems if deadlines or target dates should come and go. Who do you need to inform if a deadline is missed? Who can you rely on to pitch in if you need help? Are there backup plans if tasks are not completed at specific times? Thinking ahead might actually relieve some of the stress induced by pesky deadlines and allow you to concentrate on the task at hand.

IT'S ALL IN THE DETAILS

There are several details that could make a world of difference in the quality and appeal of your final write-up or presentation. Consider the following fine points:

The importance of the lead-in and closing statements. The tactics that you use to introduce and conclude your write-up or presentation are of the essence. Think about some of the best stories you have read or speeches you have heard. They usually engage the audience from the start with some sort of interesting and arousing impression. While you should avoid gimmicks, make an effort to come up with an attention-worthy idea that connects to the heart of your work. It may not seem fair, but your audience is likely to judge your project based on the lead-in, and may leave with only the memory of your closing.

The importance of clarity. Writing and presenting information in a clear manner is the general rule of thumb. Even the most wonderful idea can get lost in a myriad of wordiness and disorganization. You have worked hard on this project, and you want to convey the numerous features of the work, so presenting it in a clear and understandable style will be helpful to your audience. One suggestion is to start with the simple, bare aspects of your work, then go back and add detailed content and your own personality to the presentation. It is possible to combine clarity with substance so that your audience has a holistic sense of all you have accomplished.

The importance of logical sequencing. A component of your written or live presentation will be the organizational order of material as you present it. Be sure to lay out the information in a logical sequence and summarize as you go. Do not force your audience to hunt for the conclusions on their own; instead, help draw conclusions for the audience. You want your story to make sense and hold meaning for the audience, just as it has for you. Sharing the information in a rational and easy-to-follow manner can help achieve this.

Using graphs, tables, pie charts to illustrate data. As you have learned in previous chapters, highlighting the data is an important detail of your presentation. Whether your presentation is in a written or live form, using pictures to display your data is a good practice (Education Trust, 2006). You have several choices when it comes to displaying your data. The selection of the type of picture you decide to use may depend on the type of data you have or your personal preference of what seems to be easiest to read and most attractive to your audience.

Let's look at the data illustrating the number of behavioral referrals across the fourth grade level at Anytown Elementary School in different formats. Figure 5.1 shows the data in a bar graph, Figure 5.2 in a pie chart, and Table 5.1 in tabular form.

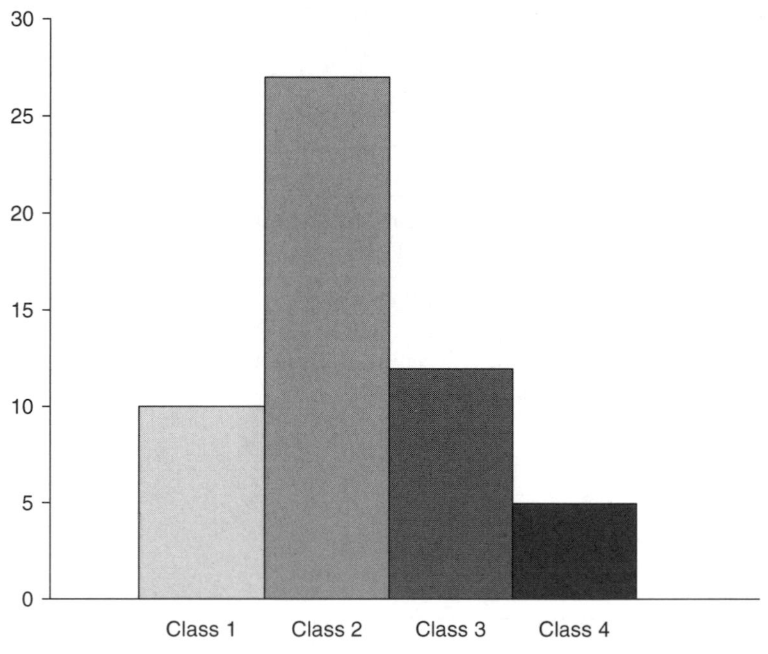

Figure 5.1 Bar Graph of Behavioral Referrals, Anytown Elementary School, Fourth Grade (2004–2005)

Use pictures, anecdotes, and quotes to bring your work to life. Think about your reasons for carrying out this project from the beginning. What sort of impact did you hope it would have and for whom? Now, how can you convey those ideas to personalize your presentation? Pictures, anecdotes, and direct quotes from participants are great ways to make these points. You are shining a light on these aspects of the work because they are what matter most. These artifacts breathe life into your hard work and show the audience the difference it has made for people in your school community.

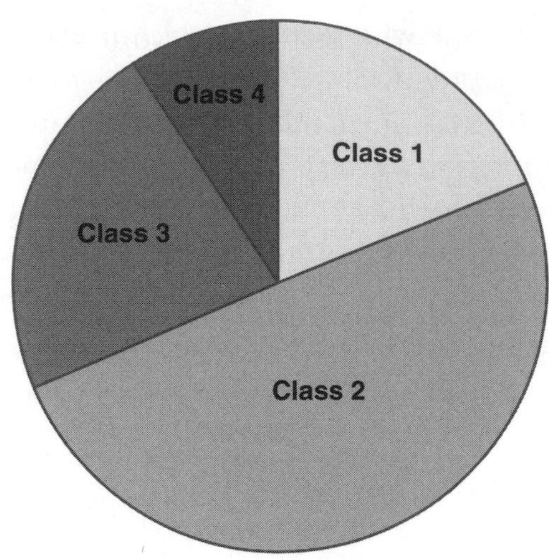

Figure 5.2 Pie Chart of Behavioral Referrals, Anytown Elementary School, Fourth Grade (2004–2005)

Table 5.1 Table of Behavioral Referrals, Anytown Elementary School, Fourth Grade (2004–2005)

Class	*Number of Referrals*
Class 1	10
Class 2	27
Class 3	12
Class 4	5

Use metaphors. If you are in the mood to get creative and want to incorporate a memorable image for your audience, consider the use of metaphors. Metaphors can help connect a picture to your work and provide a point of reference for the audience. To develop your own metaphor, ask yourself the following statement: "_____ is like _____. Just as _____ is/does _____, _____ is/does _____." For example, if your research focused on a multimethod approach to preventing dropout rates, then consider how the various methods relate to the fundamental aspects of growing a garden. Growing a garden requires a combination of factors, including sun, water, soil, and care. In your work, you used a combination of tutoring, one-on-one weekly check-ins, regular progress reports, and a study skills group to "grow" the success of your students. *The multimethod approach to decrease dropout rates* is like *growing a garden.* Just as *sun, water, soil, and care* are necessary to *grow a garden, the tutoring, weekly check-ins, progress reports, and study skills group* were necessary to *grow our students.* Using a metaphor to compare your multimethod approach to growing a garden allows your audience to see the picture and appreciate the work you have done. It is important that you do not go overboard with the use of metaphors; instead use them sparingly in the places that you really want to emphasize. Look for other ways to create metaphors and have fun as you capture the image of your work.

Prepare yourself for the audience. As you communicate, you can naturally expect some sort of response from the audience. Be on top of the possibilities by considering some obvious details. Be open to feedback that could provide some helpful ideas for your work. Others may have interesting and supportive suggestions for improvement to add to your work. Be gracious in accepting feedback from others; even if you may disagree or dislike the feedback, consider its merit. Be prepared for questions that might come from an eager audience. Listen carefully to the question, ask for clarification if necessary, and reply as best you can based on what you know. Practicing your presentation may also help you prepare. With a written document, have others look at your drafts before you put together a final version. With live presentations, conduct a run-through of your act with a few selected associates who can provide pointers to improve your final presentation. Last, be sure to relax (stretch, breathe, take a break!) as you put together this last piece. Keep yourself healthy and positive as you work toward this final step in completing your project.

As you step up to present your work, think about the strategies you want to use and the main components of your work that you want to highlight. Consider multiple ways to communicate your work, perhaps writing a report to share with your school district and then converting it to a live presentation to the school staff during an in-service opportunity. Do not rule out publishing your work. Even though it may seem ambitious, with some added effort and review your work could be in a journal or magazine. The bottom line is that you have done such good work; how can you reach as many audiences, in as many ways, to let others know about the efforts going on in your school? Go ahead, tell the world about it!

Dianne Seeks Support From Key People

So with whom could Dianne share the data that could help in developing strategies for intervention and hopefully long-term prevention? Dianne knew from the start of her project that she would need the support of several key people in her school along with the administrator. These included the literacy specialist, the ELL specialist, and the learning specialist. Thus began the support group that would help plan and strategize possible interventions. As sometimes happens in schools, changes in personnel over time meant Dianne had to communicate the project's goals to several new people. The new members were as excited and committed to the project as the longstanding members.

Remember in Chapter 2 Dianne had some questions about whom she could enlist as community partners? She knew the importance of connecting with the community if the interventions were going to be successful. The team set up a meeting with the apartment complex managers and the liaison to Community Partners for Affordable Housing. In the meeting, they shared the troubling data of the high percentage of failing students residing in the apartment complexes. Not to focus on negatives, the team continually reinforced the school's high academic expectations for and confidence in these students. One strategy that seemed to be feasible and have exciting potential was to expand and restructure the homework club. Brainstorming topics included how to recruit tutors, where the homework club could meet, who could serve as supervisors, what materials were necessary for effective tutoring (e.g., books, paper/pencils), where to obtain the educational materials, and how to inform and garner support from parents. (More on parent involvement appears in the Ongoing Case Study section of Chapter 6.) Caring, committed stakeholders brainstormed potential strategies for helping the apartment complex students become successful in school. Everyone was excited and agreed to do their assigned part before the next meeting. The improved homework club idea would be shared with other school professionals, members of the community, and several key apartment complex parents. It was happening!

6 Building Your Learning Community

Laura Pedersen

There are two reassuring thoughts to keep in mind when contemplating a practitioner inquiry project in your school. The first is that you do not have to go it alone. Being a change agent does not mean that you have to bear all the burden, nor do you have to single-handedly convince the community that your plan is the only way to go. All action research should be a collaborative undertaking in which many voices and perspectives are included and in which responsibility is shared among all participants.

The second reassurance is that you already have the skills necessary to mobilize the school community, regardless of whether or not you see yourself as a leader. The basic skills needed to build your learning community are similar to those you already use in your everyday work, only applied in a broader context. You do not have to start from scratch; you merely have to look differently at your own communication skills and problem-solving abilities. In other words, capitalize on the skills you learned in your preservice preparation.

The creation of a learning community, and its relationship to conducting practitioner inquiry, are part of a broader examination of what it means to be a professional school counselor. If our responsibility is to be agents of change and ensure that all children have equal access to the best possible education, then the learning community is the framework, and practitioner inquiry is the mechanism for forward movement (see Box Tips 6.1).

Box Tips 6.1 Essential Vocabulary

Learning Community: A school community whose philosophy is based on regular examination of daily work, the use of data to inform decisions, and continual efforts for improvement.

Stakeholder Assets: The skills, attitudes, resources, and influence that various community members have that might be utilized in the quest for positive change.

Inquiry Support Group: Team members who have an interest in the area of the research question, a stake in the outcome of the project, and an active role in some aspect of the project

Shared Leadership: All participants in a learning community have equal responsibility, equal voice, and equal commitment to the outcome. Individuals have different strengths to contribute to the project, but all have ownership of the process.

LEARNING COMMUNITIES

Helping form your learning community. Memphis, Tennessee has been proactive in promoting the role of school counselors, not only as leaders, but also as members of the community charged with fostering conditions for change in the schools. "At every school, a counselor has been assigned to assume a leadership role in (a) creating readiness for systemic change, (b) helping develop mechanisms for mapping, analyzing, and redeploying relevant school resources, and (c) working to strengthen connections between school, home, and other community resources" (Taylor & Adelman, 2000, p. 302). In this situation, there is an identified individual in each school who is the go-to person for generating support, ideas, and resources for change.

In partnership with your administrator, think about your school and ask yourself, Is this a true learning community, and do all members share leadership in the mission of the school? The learning community is based on a shared philosophy. The beliefs shared by this group about students and their potential are common threads binding the community. Do members of your school believe all children can succeed in a challenging educational environment and each member of the community has a direct impact on this achievement?

Modeling, educating and inspiring your colleagues to embrace these beliefs may seem like a daunting task. Keep in mind change takes time and sometimes it is best to start with small steps (see Box Tips 6.2). Begin by identifying a few energized or excited individuals. By maintaining focus on student outcomes (and aligning with the school improvement plan [SIP]), all members of the school community can see how their roles fit into the change process. A groundswell of support will soon begin to grow.

The need for encouragement and support is essential as communities begin to tap their resources for change. There is little hope for success if individual staff members feel they are being asked to do more with no additional resources or incentives. It is vital to recognize that encouragement and support can come in many forms: release time for planning and teaming, financial support from grants, district or school monies to facilitate trainings, and consultation and/or collaboration with local colleges and universities. Groups can be formed to provide regular engagement and feedback for those wanting to examine daily practices and to work more reflectively.

Box Tips 6.2 Forming Your Learning Community

1. Ensure that building and district administrators are integrally involved in change efforts.
2. Relate all efforts directly to improved student achievement and the school improvement plan.
3. Discuss the relationship between the change process and the school mission.
4. Use data to support decisions (e.g., failure rates, graduation rates, and other indicators of student behaviors and achievement).
5. Maintain a focus on school reform and accountability.
6. Look to schools where the change process has been successful (e.g., Chenoweth, 2007).
7. Consider using public forums with families and community groups because support for change can come from many different sources.

Looking Beyond Your School. How do you include members of the larger community into the school's learning community? "Minimally, formal efforts to create school, home, and community collaborations involve building relationships to connect and mobilize resources (e.g., financial and social capital) to enhance effectiveness and cost-efficiency" (Taylor & Adelman, 2000, p. 298). There is a plethora of possibilities for involving community individuals in the learning community. Business leaders have a vested interest in current students both as future employees and as consumers. You can begin to make these connections via parents who are in the business community. They can help generate support and make recommendations for potential members. You could also consider small business owners, business alliance members, chamber of commerce members, and industrial leaders. Your school might already have relationships with some of these through career development programs or community service programs, so broadening these relationships can be a natural progression.

Service organizations are another fertile field for identifying potential members. Examples include fraternal organizations, volunteer associations, veterans, retired citizens' groups, and community action groups. These groups often look for ways to serve in the school community. Again, you might consider checking in with parents who have knowledge and networking abilities within these groups.

Youth organizations, which are likely to serve the same children in your school, social service organizations, and municipal programs for children, can be excellent resources when you are building the learning community. You may learn that these organizations see many of the same problems and issues in their daily work with youth and families, albeit from different perspectives. Thus, the individuals within these organizations can be natural choices for the learning community.

School-community partnerships can be incredibly rewarding, offer renewal, and multiply the number of resources to help your school pursue high academic achievement for all students. Including community voices in your school's learning community can provide diverse insight, perspective, and problem-solving capacities that reach far beyond your school's walls.

Asset Mapping. Once you have identified your learning community members, consider capitalizing on their strengths or assets. One particular strategy for identifying stakeholders' assets is asset mapping. This strategy grows out of a community development model but has great relevance for school communities as well. Asset mapping is an examination of the strengths and abilities of individuals. The best way to begin addressing change is the knowledge of what assets you have at hand (Beaulieu, 2002). Asset mapping is founded on the belief that everyone has something to contribute, regardless of age, socioeconomic status, ethnicity, language, or gender. Individuals are invited to list their strengths, talents, and interests without regard to a particular project or cause.

You can develop a simple questionnaire requesting information about specific skills or talents, previous group participation (e.g., community, family, hobby, faith community), and interest in school projects. The information gathered from this process can be a resource for projects throughout the year. You may also find it helpful to identify individuals who would be interested in academic, personal, social, or career development issues and projects.

PRACTITIONER INQUIRY SUPPORT TEAM

Forming the Team. While the process of creating a learning community is based on a foundational philosophy, forming a practitioner inquiry support team is a short-term and goal-directed process. The practitioner inquiry team is the collection of people who are assembled to address a particular problem or issue. These are the people you will ask to help you examine your data, ask difficult and hard questions about the data, and brainstorm potential solutions (see Box Tips 6.3).

What voices and resources need to be included? Once you have your problem identified, defined, and illustrated by data, you must decide whom to include in brainstorming intervention strategies. Who has the skills, connections, drive, commitment, or resources to add to your efforts? Look first to your learning community membership. There are probably members from many different constituencies: teachers, parents, administrators, and community members. Consider including differing points of view. "When recruiting team members, actively seek those who don't typically volunteer, attend school functions, or hold leadership roles in the community. Choose team members who have regular and consistent contact with those they represent so they can accurately present the views of their peers, speak knowledgeably on their behalf, and take issues and action items back to them" (Ellis & Hughes, 2002, p. 2).

Box Tips 6.3 Forming a Practitioner Inquiry Support Team

1. Who, from the learning community, is accessible, willing and committed to the outcome?
2. Who, beyond the learning community, will be able to provide a positive contribution?
3. How many people are needed to provide diverse perspectives while adding strength to the team?
4. Who will be able to provide resources?

Some important considerations in identifying potential team members are (1) interest in the problem or issue, (2) stake in the outcome, and (3) full participation in the time commitment. These are all obvious considerations. Yet we tend to immediately think of those who always volunteer. Think outside the box and look for individuals who can bring diverse and multiple perspectives to the situation. Consider not only the head of the parent-teacher association but also the parent whose child has been directly affected by the problem or issue. Other considerations for membership include administrators who reflect the school's commitment to serving students effectively and students with firsthand experience of the issue.

Lead teachers or those with seniority not only provide a grounded perspective but also model for other staff members the importance of participation in practitioner inquiry and being reflective about one's own practice. The teachers who volunteer for many things can bring wonderful energy and enthusiasm to the project. However, you might also consider those on the staff or faculty who are less inclined to volunteer yet are working intimately with the issue at hand.

Last, consider individuals who can provide specific resources. Is there a building or central district administrator who has the authority to provide release time, a common planning period for group members, access to specific data, or funds to support the work of the group? Will you need additional sources of funding, reimbursement for summer or off-load work, or technological support for group members? If so, who could possibly provide assistance? Are there community members who could contribute goods or services and whose organizations might be able to provide manpower, training, or mentoring?

Prudence should also be exercised when considering the size of the team. It is important to have enough membership in your practitioner inquiry support team that diverse opinions are presented and included in the conversation; yet a large group can lead to logistical issues such as scheduling the meetings. Use your knowledge of strategies for successful groups and try to keep your core team membership between six and ten individuals.

You will also need to be realistic when sharing with members the estimation of time that will be required of participants. How many meetings, over how many weeks or months, and how much additional individual work might be asked of participants? In your enthusiasm for creating the team, be careful not to underestimate the commitment of time needed to complete the work. Less than honest estimation can result in the loss of credibility, thus jeopardizing your future work with these individuals.

Characteristics of Your School. As a final note, think about your school's ability to welcome and include team members from broad and varied backgrounds. Does the school offer parking for families and volunteers or transportation for those without a means of getting to school? Is there a welcoming space for families and visitors, access to libraries and computers, affordable childcare, and a network of translators? "Even though some obstacles are family based and some are school based, schools can play a major role in breaking the psychological barriers that have been keeping family and community members away" (Ellis & Hughes, 2002, p. 37). It is the responsibility of the school to facilitate family involvement by ensuring that families feel welcomed and by planning the logistics of school activities in such a manner that it is easy for families to participate.

Sharing Your Journey. Perhaps one of the most important things you can do is publicize ongoing collaborative efforts between the school and the community. Sharing the processes of reflection, revision, and renewed attempts can be contagious. Make sure positive change is publicized and celebrated throughout the community and emerging efforts are also shared and acknowledged. The personal as well as the professional outcomes of the work are worthy of community-wide recognition. Practitioner inquiry teams can be important contributors to professional rejuvenation and a renewed sense of purpose and energy for all individuals.

Learning communities are environments in which individuals can flourish, focus on growth and improvement, and provide students with every opportunity for success. At the same time, the practitioner inquiry team can become a mechanism whereby adults come together to better serve students and, during this process, experience their own professional growth. In a learning community focused on the success of all students, the students, families, and staff have a common vocabulary for change, an orientation toward collaboration, and a unified commitment to improvement. When all members of a learning community take on active roles in leadership and engage in examination of their daily work, the school becomes a place where anything is possible. All children really can achieve to high standards!

Dianne Brings Parents Into the Learning Community

So how did Dianne engage the learning community in the apartment complex journey? The school faculty and staff were all committed to the school improvement plan that included increasing students' academic achievement. However, up to this point Dianne had not been included on the school leadership team. Because of her work with the data and commitment to developing positive intervention strategies, the principal soon made her an integral member of the team.

As you recall, the support team and Dianne shared the data with the apartment complex managers and the liaison from the Community Partners for Affordable Housing Association. One of the conversations during this meeting included how to inform and gather parental support. A forum for parents was developed. Dinner was provided and you guessed it: The turnout was huge! At the forum, Dianne and the team shared the qualities necessary for children to become high-achieving students. A key essential ingredient: completing and turning in homework! Students who do not have mastery of the material can still be successful because we will provide help at the complex.

Parents began to have hope for their child's success. Energy was being generated! Residents talked about using the apartment community center for the restructured afterschool homework club. Dianne worked with the manager of the center and new life was breathed into the homework club! Community Partners helped identify tutors at the middle and high schools. Community groups donated snacks for the students participating in the club. Teachers and the team provided materials and guidance for tutors. Tutors were trained in homework support strategies as well as how to contact and connect with classroom teachers. Amazing at it may seem, the complex parents soon developed a permission form for tenants to sign allowing the tutors to *directly* contact teachers! Excitement and support for the project were growing by the month.

Tutors were being seen as integral players in the children's success at schools. They soon found themselves called on to help in other areas of the children's lives (e.g., bus referrals, asking for help). Dianne's original project had taken on a life of its own! She had woven her knowledge and skills into the big picture of how to succeed in school—and life. Through parent education and tutor education, she and the team were able to share information and expertise enhancing multiple aspects of the children's lives.

When the school's learning community heard about the great work being done in the apartment complexes, they began to look differently at the work being conducted in their own building. Soon colleagues began to strategize and implement in-school help for the students, including pulling out those who need more specialized assistance, individualizing testing for those needing help, training community adults as tutoring assistants, and providing small-group testing areas and additional learning programs. Academic support strategies were popping up both in and out of school. Her support team had grown from a few select learning community members to the apartment complex manager, adult tutoring coordinators, student tutors, and community business alliances. It works!

7 Review and Can-Do

Putting It All Together

Our intentions with this book were to provide suggestions for each step of the inquiry process, with the goal of helping you gain skills and leave you with a sense of accomplishment about the work you do with students. We also wanted to point out the multiple layers associated with practitioner inquiry: you are impacting your school environment to an extent that you may not have realized before. Whether you utilized this book as a whole, or referred to individual chapters for your most immediate interests, we hope that we have introduced new ways of exploring issues in your school. We leave you with our hopes and ideas for you, the reader.

We hope that we have sparked a new sense of curiosity.

You have so many good ideas to explore already! Think about all the questions you (and others) have been asking, the hints all around you, and the hypotheses that have been brewing in your head for a while. Now is the time to explore those ideas and take the next steps to find the missing pieces that will tell the whole story. In Chapter 1, we discussed the art of inquiry and strategies for turning those ideas into questions. The content of Chapter 2 encourages you to find additional information that might expand your initial idea and set you on a path toward solutions and positive changes for your students.

We hope that we have helped you sharpen your observational skills.

As school counselors, you have eyes and ears in places that others may not. You have the training and expertise to gather evidence from various sources, put it together as a whole, and significantly impact your school. Chapters 3 and 4 were written to help guide you to the people and places that have the information to address your question. You can find help in answering your question from anywhere—from expert educators, colleagues in your school, technology resources, the data that already exists, and so on. The answers and solutions may be closer than you realize. You are the one who can uncover and describe the data and bring along others who, like you, are looking toward new solutions.

We hope that we have conveyed the importance of good communication.

Throughout the book, we have stressed that you are not alone in this process. The practitioner inquiry process is more enjoyable and more effective when those conducting it work as a team. Chapter 6 offered ideas for getting others on board and identified those people who might provide valuable insight into your tasks. Following school protocol, involving those with particular expertise, and conducting ongoing check-ins are always critical steps when venturing into school improvement territory. Chapter 5 explored fundamental avenues of communicating your work to others, namely writing and presenting your work. Tips for organizing, strategizing, and completing it all were reviewed. We know that you have great ideas to share, and hope that you now have new ideas for communicating them at every stage of the inquiry process from beginning to end.

We hope that we have provided a new and important context for the work you do.

By conceptualizing your work as a contribution to educational equity, you should be proud that your inquiry ideas are part of something bigger. Your ideas may spur changes in everyday practice that generate possibilities for students that they never considered before. Thinking from the perspective of practitioner inquiry allows you to see the layers of impact that you can have—on individual students, on groups of students, on the whole school, on the whole district—as a member of a significant profession who is doing their part. Beginning your work with the "big picture" attitude may inspire and motivate you in new ways.

We hope that we have encouraged a sense of confidence.

Along the way in reading this book, we figure that you have noticed that there is no magic in the pages—you have the practical tools and abilities to take an idea and run with it, creating ideas and solutions for bettering the services your school has to offer. There are tidbits of information that you can use at every stage of your practitioner inquiry work, with realistic suggestions that you can start doing now. The beauty of practitioner inquiry is that it has to make sense only for *your* school, using the information and ideas that arise from *your* community to make positive changes for *your* students. It is not a one-size-fits-all formula, because all schools are different. Identifying and meeting the needs of your school is the mission, and we know that you are up for it.

Where's Dianne Now?

Dianne's story is an exciting one to share. The success helps make the story, but key to the success was the teaming and collaboration between individuals and organizations who all agreed on one central issue: the apartment complexes' students needed help to become academically successful in school. As of this book's publication, the interventions set forth by the teams both inside and outside of the school continue to help bolster all students' academic success.

In Dianne's words, "The original data journey led to a more comprehensive program for all kids—less patchwork and more preventive measures. Interventions needed to be systemic, systematic, and preventive." As her role in academic interventions continued to grow, Dianne made sure she regularly supported and updated the team and principal. Her professional position within the school began to change. She moved to a new office location, central in the building rather than in the ancillary wing. Colleagues no longer viewed her as an individual who worked only one-on-one with students. Dianne was now a key player in helping all stakeholders develop and implement successful interventions for all students.

As in most cases of change, there has been resistance. However, the team's collaborative work in making decisions has helped dissuade those who were skeptical. Data can speak very loudly, and in this case, it did! The yearly increase in the school's state test scores has garnered an exceptional rating for the school (see Table 7.1). Wow! It began with the counselor's initial question, combined with the principal's support, which led to the formation of a team to work with the community at large and the apartment complexes to all achieve the goal of increasing the academic success of the students.

Often we say to ourselves: I think there's a problem, but there's too much on my plate right now; I just don't see where I can find the time. Step back, look at your discerning piece of data, and ask some simple questions: What are the risks of nonaction? How many students could be affected? How many could continue to be minimized, left out, fail or drop out? If these questions and their answers are uncomfortable for you, you have the answer: Action is necessary.

Take the risk, ask the difficult questions, and see where it leads you and your team. It could be as exciting a journey as Dianne's has been over the past six years. Central to your success will be taking the *m* in me and turning it upside down to make the *w* in *we*! Good luck, and please share your stories with us and others. We know your work can make a difference in the academic and career success of students—and, ultimately, in the quality of their lives.

Table 7.1 Year Summary Data: Third-Grade Year-End Test Scores

Subject	*Year*	*Total Number Tested*	*Total Number Failing*
Math	2000–2001	200	62
Reading		196	37
Math	2001–2002	184	30
Reading		184	37
Math	2002–2003	197	28
Reading		199	36
Math	2003–2004	210	18
Reading		210	20
Math	2004–2005	186	11
Reading		184	2
Math	2005–2006	189	15
Reading		187	9

References

American School Counselor Association. (2005). *ASCA national model: A framework for school counseling programs* (2nd ed.). Alexandria, VA: Author.

Armstrong, T. (1994). Multiple intelligences: Seven ways to approach curriculum. *Educational Leadership, 52,* 26–28.

Bauman, S. (2004). School counselors and research revisited. *Professional School Counseling, 7*(3), 141–151.

Beaulieu, L. J. (2002). *Mapping the assets of your community: A key component for building local capacity*. Mississippi State, MS: Southern Rural Development Center. (ERIC Document Reproduction Service No. ED 467309)

Brown, D., & Trusty, J. (2005). School counselors, comprehensive school counseling programs, and academic achievement: Are school counselors promising more than they can deliver? *Professional School Counseling, 9*(1), 1–8.

Chenoweth, K. (2007). *It's being done: Academic success in unexpected schools.* Cambridge, MA: Harvard Education Press.

Crawford, M., & Doughterty, E. (2003). *Updraft/downdraft: Secondary schools in the crosswinds of reform*. Lanham, MD: Scarecrow Education.

Dunn, R., & Stevenson, J. M. (1997). Teaching diverse college students to study with a learning-styles prescription. *College Student Journal, 31,* 333–339.

Education Trust National Center for Transforming School Counseling. (2006). *Systemic school counseling: A blueprint for student success.* Module 1. Washington, DC: National Author.

Ellis, D., & Hughes, K. (2002). *Partnership by design: Cultivating effective and meaningful school-family-community partnerships.* Portland, OR: Northwest Regional Educational Library.

Gardner, H. (2006). *Multiple intelligences: New horizons.* New York: Basic Books.

Hagstrom, D. (2004). *From outrageous to inspired: how to build a community of leaders in our schools*. San Francisco: Jossey-Bass.

Hubbard, R., & Power, B. (2003). *The art of classroom inquiry: a handbook for teacher-researchers*. Portsmouth, NH: Heinemann.

Johnson, R. S. (2002). *Using data to close the achievement gap: how to manage equity in our schools.* Thousand Oaks, CA: Corwin Press.

Klassen, S. (2005). *Using data tip sheet: template for trainings.* Unpublished manuscript. Available by contacting the author at klasjan@comcast.net.

Mahlum, L. (2002). *Reflective Journal Writing.* Unpublished manuscript, Lewis & Clark College.

Martin, I. (2002). *Reflective Journal Writing.* Unpublished manuscript, Lewis & Clark College.

Matteri, S. A. (2005). *Promoting college through the PSAT.* Unpublished manuscript, Lewis & Clark College.

Rowell, L. L. (2005). Collaborative action research and school counselors. *Professional School Counseling, 9*(1), 28–36.

Rowell, L. L. (2006). Action research and school counseling: Closing the gap between research and practice. *Professional School Counseling, 9*(5), 376–384.

Sagor, R. (2005). *The action research guidebook: A four-step process for educators and school teams.* Thousand Oaks, CA: Corwin Press.

Schorr, L. B. (1997). *Common purpose: Strengthening families and neighborhoods to rebuild America.* New York: Bantam Doubleday Dell.

Sink, C. A. (Ed.). (2006). Research methods in school counseling [Special issue]. *Professional School Counseling, 9*(5).

Stone, C. B., & Dahir, C. A. (2004). *School counselor accountability: A MEASURE of student success.* Upper Saddle River, NJ: Pearson Education.

Swientek, A. (2002). *Reflective Journal Writing.* Unpublished manuscript, Lewis & Clark College.

Taylor, L., & Adelman, H.S. (2000). Connecting schools, families, and communities. *Professional School Counseling, 3*, 298–308.

Whiston, S. C. (2002). Response to the past, present, and future of school counseling: Raising some issues. *Professional School Counseling, 5*(3), 148–157.

RECOMMENDED RESOURCES

Bryan, J., & Holcomb-McCoy, C. (2004). School counselors' perceptions of their involvement in school-family-community partnerships. *Professional School Counseling, 7*, 162–171.

Dana, N. F., & Yendol-Silva, D. (2003). *The reflective educator's guide to classroom research: Learning to teach and teaching to learn through practitioner inquiry.* Thousand Oaks, CA: Corwin Press.

DeVoss, J. A., & Andrews, M. F. (2006). *School counselors as educational leaders.* New York: Lahaska.

Dimmitt, C., Carey, J. C., & Hatch, T. (2007). *Evidence-based school counseling: Making a difference with data-driven practices.* Thousand Oaks, CA: Corwin Press.

Holcomb-McCoy, C. (2007). *School counseling to close the achievement gap: A social justice framework for success*. Thousand Oaks, CA: Corwin Press.

House, R. M., & Hayes, R. L. (2002). School counselors: Becoming key players in school reform. *Professional School Counseling, 5*, 249–56.

Keys, S. G. (2000). Living the collaborative role: Voices from the field. *Professional School Counseling, 3*, 332–339.

Lambert, L. (2002). A framework for shared leadership. *Educational Leadership, 58*, 37–40.

Martin, P. J. (2002). Transforming school counseling: A national perspective. *Theory into Practice, 41*, 148–53.

Search Institute. (2007). [Home page]. Retrieved June 11, 2007, from http://www.search-institute.org

Smith, R. W., Ross, M., & Robichaux, R. (2004). Creation and validation of a measure of leadership density in elementary and middle schools. *Journal of Research for Educational Leader, 2*, 79–111.

Stone, C. B., & Dahir, C. A. (2006). *The transformed school counselor.* New York: Lahaska.

Index

The Corwin Press logo—a raven striding across an open book—represents the union of courage and learning. Corwin Press is committed to improving education for all learners by publishing books and other professional development resources for those serving the field of PreK–12 education. By providing practical, hands-on materials, Corwin Press continues to carry out the promise of its motto: **"Helping Educators Do Their Work Better."**